Empath Healing

How to Become a Healer and Avoid Narcissistic Abuse. The Guide to Develop your Powerful Gift for Highly Sensitive People. Emotion Healing Solution

Table of contents

Introduction

Pain is a part of our lives now. It knows no boundaries. Our lives have been saturated with pain, stress, anxiety, and grief so much that we feel the emotions burdening our chests, making strain in our souls. There is hardly anyone nowadays who isn't burdened with problems. It causes us brevity of breath and makes us jump when we focus on it.

This is the thing that it feels like to live through the worldwide change of humankind in the mid-21st century. Be it climate change, family problems, workplace issues, they are deliberations, each one of them.

Yet, the sentiment of searching for peace and comfort has become increasingly futile with the passing time. No one seems to be happy. Don't our hearts bleed when we see our near and dear ones in pain? Don't we feel like extending our hand, pulling them into a hug and tell them that everything will be fine? These things are instinctive. They are physical and present. They are going on this moment and you can feel it in your bones, yet it is equally tough to find someone to lean upon when the world is slowly becoming desensitized to the emotions. Feeling sympathy is common, while empathetic gestures are increasingly becoming uncommon.

Social developments have led to the mechanization of everything, even emotions. Everything is guarded, a lie that we tell ourselves and others. For example, take social media-- we scroll and scroll, like and comment on cute videos and emotional stories of struggling human beings. However, how many of us would reach out to others to help those who are in distress? This is the moment when we have to realize that humanity needs to be awakened again. The emotions which we have been suppressing to fit into the crowd need to burn with passion again. It is a rallying call for us to decorate their defensive layer, get our weapons, and stand up to the foe at their entryway. Our enemy is none other than our insensitivity. It needs to be taken care of. The world needs healing; it needs the touch of love and genuine empathy. It needs healers.

Unfortunately misinformed in this methodology is the inability to perceive that what the world needs now, like never before, is healing. We have long overlooked our inner feelings and while doing this we take pride in the fact that we are moving away from what is significant. Not only us; everyone around us is going through the same painful situations. There is not a bleak of hope and our existence has been put for questioning. The present is so shaky that the future cannot find a ground to build itself. Giving way to emotions and helping others is seen as a weakness. It is a misinformed fact. Those who bare their souls are and would be the one to bring stability in the chaotic environment which we are living in.

These people are called healers.

The world needs healers and we continue encircling the procedure of social change as a progression of challenges. The polarization of emotions fused with material gains is creating driving a wedge among people who are supposed to love and care for each other.

Frantically required right currently is to look in reverse in time and truly comprehend the main drivers of our misfortunes. These issues emerged in the past when our predecessors were in unfortunate associations with our environment, other individuals, and ourselves. These problems are associated with each other. They are foundational. They occurred on our watch since we aggregately feel — someplace somewhere inside — this is actually what we merit. Our answers keep on being piecemeal on the grounds that every one of us, in manners we are too hesitant to even think about admitting, is broken and doesn't have the foggiest idea how to assemble the pieces back once more.

To fix things, we do not need fights and disputes. We need to look beyond our pigeonhole and look for solutions in the astral world. Believe it or not- this is the work for healers. While doctors, scientists, and humanitarians along with others are contributing to their part, sometimes it pays to widen our thoughts and beliefs and act upon them.

It might sound curious to state that affection is the appropriate response; however, it happens to be valid.

We need stalwart love, purifying and transformative love. We have to begin accepting that we are deserving of adoration with the goal that we can fabricate a world together that conveys it for us and who and what is to come.

The problem is that we see problems as a bystander. That needs to be changed. We cannot truly understand someone's issues without opening our emotional channels and absorbing what they are feeling. We can only mend our planet by perceiving that we are an integral part of it. We cure our wrecked lives and issues by a get-together in networks and building up solid social standards for initiative and portrayal. Our financial issues can only be solved by pulling back our help from the narcissists and putting rather in important connections among individuals who help us feel supported inside.

This is the thing that has been going on in a million little pockets of mankind all through the most recent fifty years.

We don't need to hang tight for it to start. It is completely in the procedure and developing day by day. All around the globe there are individuals framing agreeable organizations, putting resources into neighborhood networks, shaping ideological groups around life and mending (to supplant those of war, victory, and passing), making new advances that improve well-being and essentialness, making it simpler to associate with others in our very own networks and traversing the globe.

Individuals share these invigorating qualities at present. You are not the only one. There is power in numbers. The more insensitive we will be, the more the world around us will crumble as there is no one to take care of anyone. We are an army and our numbers develop every day. We have to tap into that power and do our best to make this world a better place.

However, there is much work to do and time is of the substance. Be a healer in your little pocket of this incredibly vast world. Hold firm to the sentiments of appreciation and to an option that is bigger than yourself and you will most likely think back on this progress with satisfaction and a warm heart. Give the individuals who a chance to react in dread and little mindedness live with their disgrace numerous decades from now, there will be some among us whom we won't most likely help. Discover comfort realizing that you opened your heart when the living things of this world called out in agony. What's more, you felt a similar hurt in yourself, constrained in this manner to sustain and recuperate.

However, it's not easy. Empaths are seen as weak. If you are an Empath, then you will probably be the worst sufferer as others will misuse your kindness and care. Since you understand the emotions of everyone around, you might encounter someone who will bully you, and you will almost always forgive them as it's not in your nature to hold grudges. Yes, you might end up facing abuse from a narcissist.

Here in this book, you will get to know more about Empath Healing, abilities, strengths, weaknesses, and much more. This information is essential for us to embrace our true, emotional selves as that would allow clearing our biases and becoming better human beings in the process. Feeling our inner love and those of others isn't a weakness. It will build up this world. In the time when empathy is buried deep inside somewhere and shallowness is riding with its head high, healers can be the saviors. If you feel you are the one, then do not hesitate to take charge. Do not be afraid to be charitable when it comes to servicing the humankind because this is precisely what we need now. And you need to protect yourself as well because without protecting yourself you cannot help others. It is essential to take a stand for yourself or else it will be too late-- for you and the world.

Chapter 1: <u>What is Empathy?</u>

To understand empathy, you need to go through the definition of empathy in detail, as described by different disciplines. This is the moment when you can seek a helping hand to protect yourself from the abuse you are encountering.

The word "empathy" appeared about a century prior in the form of a German term Einfühlung, it's meaning signifying "feeling-in." English-talking analysts proposed a bunch of different interpretations of the word, including "liveliness," play," compassion," and "similarity." Significantly, in 1908, two clinicians from Cornell and the University of Cambridge recommended "empathy" for the German word, drawing on the Greek "em" for "in" and "sentiment" for "feeling," and it took a flight since then.

At the time the term was new, and empathy was not fundamentally a way to feel someone else's feelings, yet the exceptionally opposite. The meaning was extremely different as compared to the way we use it today. Earlier, to have compassion meant to breathe life into an item, or to extend one's own envisioned sentiments onto the world. This is similar to the "white man's burden" when the west needed to enlighten other cultures. The absolute most punctual brain research investigates compassion concentrated on "kinaesthetic empathy," a substantial inclination or development that created a feeling of converging with an article. Expressions of the human experience pundits of the 1920s asserted that with compassion, a group of spectators individuals could feel as though they were completing the conceptual developments of the defined definition of empathy.

By mid-century, the definition of empathy started to change as certain therapists directed their concentration toward the study of social relations. In 1948, the test analyst Rosalind Dymond Cartwright, in a joint effort with her humanist guide, Leonard Cottrell, directed a portion of the principal tests estimating relational empathy. All the while, she purposely dismissed empathy's initial importance of inventive projection and rather underscored relational association as the center of the idea.

In the whirlwind of trial investigations of empathy that pursued, therapists started to separate "genuine" empathy, characterized as the exact examination of another's musings or sentiments, from what they called "projection" The term further experienced a change. Empathy was then described as the capacity to value the other individual's emotions without yourself ending up so sincerely included that your judgment is influenced. This definition has gained wide usage all around the world.

In a previous couple of decades, intrigue for empathy has spread to primatology and neuroscience as well. Important research also contributed to the study and understanding of empathy. During the 1990s, neuroscientists conducting research on monkeys found mirror neurons, cells in the creatures' cerebrums that fired when a monkey moved. The most important part was that they reacted when the monkey saw another make a similar action or gesture. The disclosure of mirror neurons prodded a rush of examination into empathy and brain action that immediately stretched out to people also. Other late investigations have additionally enlarged compassion's venture into fields like financial aspects and writing, finding that riches variations debilitate empathic reaction and that perusing fiction can improve it.

Understanding Empathy

The expression "empathy" is utilized to depict a wide scope of feelings. Psychologists and researchers, for the most part, characterize empathy as the capacity to detect other individuals' feelings, combined with the capacity to envision what another person may think or feel. It additionally is the capacity to feel and share someone else's feelings. Some accept that compassion includes the capacity to coordinate another's feelings, while others accept that sympathy includes being kind toward another person.

The most important part is to make a rational decision based on what the empath is feeling for others without being emotionally affected by it.

Contemporary analysts regularly separate between two kinds of empathy. One is
"full of feeling empathy" alludes to the sensations and sentiments we get because of others' feelings. This type of empathy can incorporate understanding what another individual is feeling, or simply feeling pushed when we recognize another's dread or nervousness. "Psychological empathy," once in a while called "point of view taking," alludes to our capacity to distinguish and comprehend other individuals' feelings. Studies propose that individuals with chemical imbalance range issue experience serious difficulties identifying. Martin Hoffman is an analyst who concentrated on the improvement of compassion. As per Hoffman, everybody is brought into the world with the ability of inclination empathy.

Empathy definitions envelop a wide scope of emotional states, including thinking about other individuals and wanting to support them; encountering feelings that match someone else's feelings; observing what someone else is thinking or feeling; and making less particular the contrasts between oneself and the other. It can likewise be comprehended as having the separateness of characterizing oneself and another a blur.

Empathy supposedly has profound roots in our mind and body. The same case goes with our evolutionary history. Basic types of empathy have been seen in our primate relatives and other animals such as dogs. Empathy has been associated with two zones in our cerebrum. Researchers have found that a few fragments of empathy can be safely linked to mirror neurons. Mirror neurons are the cells in the mind that start firing when we watch another person play out an activity in the same way as we do, that they would fire on the off chance that we played out that activity ourselves. Also, recent research has additionally linked heredity to empathy; however, studies recommend that individuals can improve or restrain their normal empathetic abilities.

Having empathy doesn't really mean we will need to help anyone anytime; however, it's frequently a crucial initial move toward spreading love and comfort to help ease those who are in distress, pain or misfortune.

Types of Empathy

As indicated by analyst and pioneer in the field of emotions, Paul Ekman, Ph.D., three particular sorts of empathy have been recognized:

Subjective Empathy: Also called "point of view taking," psychological empathy is the capacity to comprehend and foresee the emotions and contemplations of others by envisioning one's self in their circumstance.

Emotional Empathy: Closely identified with psychological empathy, emotional empathy is the capacity to really feel what someone else feels or if nothing else, feel feelings like theirs. In this case, there is in every case some degree of shared sentiments. This trait can be an attribute among people who are diagnosed with mental disorders, such as Asperger's Syndrome.

Compassionate or Humane Empathy: Driven by their profound comprehension of the other individual's emotions dependent on shared encounters, mercifully empathic individuals endeavor genuine endeavors to help.

Is Empathy Sympathy?

Sympathy and empathy are terms related to compassion. Definitions have changed over the course of years. Empathy is frequently characterized as a feeling we feel when others are out of luck, which persuades us to support them. Sympathy is a sentiment of consideration and concern for somebody out of luck. Some incorporate into empathy as empathic concern, a sentiment of worry for another, where a few researchers incorporate the desire to see them happier.

Compassion is often unintentionally equated with pity. Pity is an inclination that one feels towards others that may be in a tough situation or needing assistance as they can't fix their issues themselves, regularly portrayed as feeling bad for somebody.

Since compassion means understanding the emotional conditions of other individuals, the manner in which it is portrayed is gotten from the manner in which feelings themselves are described. In the event that, for instance, feelings are taken to be midway portrayed by real sentiments, at that point getting a handle on the real sentiments of another will be vital to empathy. Then again, if feelings are all the more midway portrayed by a blend of convictions and want, at that point getting a handle on these convictions and wants will be increasingly basic to empathy. The capacity to envision yourself as someone else is a refined creative procedure, which a lot of us confuse with the feelings of pity. Be that as it may, the fundamental ability to perceive feelings is presumably innate and might be accomplished unknowingly. However, it tends to be trained and accomplished with different degrees of force or precision.

Sympathy fundamentally has a "pretty much" quality. The worldview instance of an empathic connection, in any case, includes an individual conveying a precise acknowledgment of the criticality of someone else's progressing purposeful activities, related emotional states, and individual attributes in a way that the perceived individual can bear that. Acknowledgments that are both exact and middle of the road are focal highlights of empathy.

The human ability to perceive the substantial sentiments of another is identified with one's imitative limits and is by all accounts grounded in an intrinsic ability to relate the real developments and outward appearances one finds in another with the proprioceptive sentiments of creating those comparing developments or articulations oneself. Humans appear to make the equivalent quick association between the manner of speaking and other vocal articulations and internal inclination.

In Positive Psychology, sympathy has likewise been contrasted and charitableness and self-love. Selflessness is conduct that is planned for profiting someone else, while conceit is a conduct that is carried on for individual addition. Here and there, when somebody is feeling sympathetic towards someone else, demonstrations of selflessness happen. Notwithstanding, many inquiries whether these demonstrations of benevolence are roused by boastful increases. As per constructive analysts, individuals can be sufficiently moved by their emotions to be altruistic, and there are other people who think about inappropriate good points of view and having sympathy can prompt polarization, lead to viciousness and may cause 25066conduct seeing someone.

For example, you can feel pity for a beggar and even give them some money. But that's it. Going beyond "just giving money" and helping other people out of their miserable state is what empathy embodies. Teaching underprivileged children with a vision to make their future bright is empathy. Just giving attendance in the classroom and barely teaching is not. If someone is distraught or sick, staging an intervention is empathy, feeling pity is not. There are so many examples which can be given. Our world is full of them.

Here, what is important is to truly feel and do the needful action which not only gives you solace but benefits others as well. All of us watch videos where someone helped an animal out and rehabilitated them. Animal rescuers are the best example of empaths. Animals cannot pay anyone back in cash but in kind. Rescuing them is a shining indication of what empathy should look like. Those who go beyond wanting material benefits for themselves and help others genuinely are the pioneers of kindness which our world needs so critically now.

Chapter 2: Empathy Theories Straight from the Scientific Arena

A lot of research has been conducted on empathy. Mostly, the neuroscience and human's primitive social behaviors have been taken into consideration to understand the nuances of empathy. The theories mentioned below are results of several years of hard work scientists have invested in contemplating the sensitive side of human beings, and why some humans are more sensitive and receptive to others.

Hoffman's on empathy through the twentieth century is explained well in the developmental by therapist Martin L. Hoffman (2000), whose hypothesis of moral improvement has given the most exhaustive perspective on empathy. Hoffman mainly focuses on empathic trouble in his works. His hypothesis incorporates five ways to clarify how one becomes bothered when watching another person's trouble. The five methods are mimicry, classical conditioning, direct association, mediated affiliation, and role-taking. In Hoffman's (2000) initial three instruments, the eyewitness sees the subject's emotional experience legitimately. These instruments are viewed as crude, programmed, and automatic.

Mimicry. Empathizing through mimicry is a two-way process. To begin with, the onlooker naturally observes the objective's emotional facial, postural, or vocal articulations. Second, input from the imitated expressions causes the related emotional response in the eyewitness. For instance, if someone was bitten by a stray dog, you will unconsciously imitate their emotions. Your very own feeling of dread makes you feel frightened as well. This impersonation procedure of mimicry is the thing that Hatfield, Cacioppo, and Rapson (1994) called it primitive emotional contagion.

Classical conditioning. Classical conditioning of emotions starts with circumstances that make us feel emotional regardless of whether we have never experienced them. For instance, you may feel frightened when the dog bites you. After you experience the inherently emotion-inducing circumstance, we discover that specific signals are an indication that it is going to happen once more. Therefore, we begin to feel anxious when we see those dogs. You may discover that those dogs snarl before they run after you to bite; thus you start to feel terrified when you hear a dog snarl. In the language of classical conditioning, the dog bite is an unconditioned stimulus (UCS) that makes you feel frightened as an unconditioned reaction (UCR); the canine snarl is the neutral stimulus (NS) that is associated with the dog bite frequently enough to turn into a conditioned stimulus (CS) that makes you feel frightened as a conditioned reaction (CR).

Here, the thought is that others' emotional encounters can trigger a conditioned emotional reaction. In one variant of traditionally adapted empathy, during conditioning, we experience unconditioned stimulus (UCS's) with other people who are communicating feelings (NS's). This matching of the circumstance and others' emotional articulations makes the emotion-inducing articulations the prompts (CS's) that a comparative circumstance is going to happen. Therefore, others' emotional articulations cause us to feel emotions (CRs), which we experience as compassion. For instance, you may see a stray animal try to attack someone else who looks terrified (NS) directly before a similar canine assault you (UCS) and you feel apprehensive (UCR). Later on, when you see others' fear responses (CS), you will feel apprehensive once more (CR).

In the main form, the objective's emotional reaction causes empathic feelings, though in the second form highlights of the objective's emotional situation which causes empathic feelings.

Direct association. In this case, when the eyewitness sees the objective's emotional response or circumstance, it reminds the eyewitness of their own past emotional encounters. At that point, the eyewitness feels the feelings that they felt during the first encounters. For instance, on the off chance that you see a stray dog attacking someone, at that point you may recall when an animal assaulted you. You reexperience the first fear from the memory.

Mediated affiliation. In this case, onlookers find out about targets' emotional encounters through words. At that point, onlookers envision the objectives' emotional responses and copy them, recollect their own past encounters and feel the feelings from the recollections or both. This affiliation is like mimicry or direct affiliation however the eyewitness does not see the objective's experience in a direct manner.

Role taking. Role taking happens when eyewitnesses either envision themselves in the other person's circumstance or envision how they feel. Similarly, as with mediated affiliation, onlookers may copy envisioned emotional responses or might feel emotions by utilizing their emotional recollections to envision the objective's circumstance. By and by, role-taking is more tedious than mediated affiliation. It includes dynamic endeavors to comprehend an objective by bringing emotional recollections or imagined emotional articulations to mind, though intervened affiliation includes an increasingly programmed initiation of enthusiastic recollections or symbolism.

Hoffman talks about mimicry, direct affiliation, mediated affiliation, and role-taking as independent systems for empathy even in spite of the fact that they are put in the same category. For every one of them, the spectator's emotional experience originates from emulating emotional responses or reviewing emotional memories. The distinctions are whether the spectator must watch the objective's feeling or circumstance legitimately (mimicry and direct affiliation) or can construe them in a roundabout way (intervened affiliation and role-taking) and whether the eyewitness places in some push to empathize (taking) or not (the other four).

In his depiction of role-taking, Hoffman expresses that onlookers can envision the subject's emotional circumstance so clearly that they feel a similar feeling. This is the main case where Hoffman says that empathy probably won't depend on related knowledge or a context-free natural component (mimicry) and it starts to seem like an ordinary emotional experience. On the off chance that a spectator can feel the feeling by distinctively envisioning the objective's circumstances, at that point for what reason couldn't the spectator feel the feeling by straightforwardly seeing the objective's circumstance? Are the memory-based and mimicry components vital for sympathy?

Emotion theory

A baseline of emotion hypothesis is that feeling is a programmed system that is developed to manage flexible behavior. Emotion is additionally, be that as it may, a method for relational correspondence that brings out reactions from different people and situations. In this manner, feelings can be considered both to be intrapersonal and social states, and the development of empathy combines both such estimations and mirrors an intersubjective acknowledgment process which is helpful in sorting unfavorable emotions. Without rejecting it, a lot of research has been done on informative science, brain research, and emotion neuroscience. Collectively, they have blended together to define empathy as a characteristic competency that has developed in our brains to create and maintain social bonds, important for enduring, reproducing and keeping up prosperity.

These various segments include—

- Affective sharing is the primary component of empathy. This type of empathy reflects a person's capability to absorb the vibrations of others and feel energized by their valence and power of emotions.

- Empathic understanding revolves around the concept of in-depth attention to the emotional state of someone.

- Empathic concern, which alludes to the inspiration to think about somebody's well-being genuinely.

- Cognitive empathy is characterized by knowing, understanding, or appreciating on a scholarly level. As the majority of us know, to comprehend trouble isn't a similar thing as feeling miserable or sad.

Considering the multifaceted segments of compassion (or empathy, as we call it), there is no single locale in the cerebrum that underlies this limit. Or on the other hand, possibly, the neural system related with the dorsolateral prefrontal cortex, parietal cortex, and brainstem, operational hub, basal ganglia, and ventromedial prefrontal cortex- build up self-sufficient and firmly developed biological frameworks that help us in experiencing empathy. Additionally, the neural pathways included compassion and care are empowered and balanced by neuroendocrine frameworks. If we look at, in particular, the neuropeptide oxytocin initiates social relationships. It does so by diminishing stress and apprehension, and along these lines improves cognitive empathy.

Simulation Theory

Simulation Theory, says that empathy is conceivable on the grounds that when we see someone else encountering a feeling, we "recreate" or speak to that equivalent feeling in ourselves so we can know first-hand what it feels like. Actually, there is some fundamental proof of supposed mirror neurons in people that fire during both the perception and experience of activities and feelings. Also, there are even parts of the cerebrum in the prefrontal cortex (in charge of higher-level sorts of information) that show the cover of initiation for both self-engaged and other-centered thoughts and decisions. On an instinctive level, Simulation Theory bodes well, since it appears to be extremely clear that so as to comprehend what someone else is feeling. Notwithstanding its natural intrigue, Simulation Theory must be tried to perceive what proof exists for it in the mind.

The other proposed hypothesis that endeavors to understand empathy, which a few specialists think totally contradicts. Simulation Theory is known as the Theory of Mind-the capacity to comprehend what someone else is thinking and feeling dependent on principles for how one should think and feel. Research investigating Theory of Mind has turned out to be exceptionally famous in clinical work on neurotransmitter imbalance; the essential research demonstrating that medically introverted people can't viably speak to or clarify the psychological conditions of another. All the more as of late, errands those Tap Theory of Mind procedures have been executed in brain scans. The outcomes from these investigations demonstrate that there might be explicit cerebrum territories that underlie and bolster a Theory of Mind.

What's in all likelihood, possibly, is that empathy is a multi-faceted emotion, with certain parts of it being increasingly programmed and passionate (quickly getting agitated when we see a friend or family member who's disturbed) and different parts of it that are progressively intelligent and calculated (understanding why somebody may be angry or pissed-off depending on what we think about the individual, their character, and so on). Regardless of whether the more programmed or the more intelligent viewpoint "kicks in" will fundamentally rely upon the social setting wherein we get ourselves. This is an overwhelming, open inquiry, and we will need to sit tight for social neuroscience as a field to grow more and address it.

For the present, what we can say from compassion research is that we have started to see how the mind offers to ascend to the great limit we need to "feel into" another person. With the freshly discovered instruments of social neuroscience close by, therapists and neuroscientists are currently on the cusp of more disclosures about the empathic existence of the empathic cerebrum.

Social Baseline Theory

Social help is one of the most significant elements of social connections. Various researches have shown that it is basic for keeping up physical and psychological well-being, and an absence of help is related to not-so-good outcomes. An abundance of proof recommends that accessibility of a loved one or family or companions' support, by and large, eases stress and is related to well-being and prosperity. Then again, an absence of help and social detachment are significant indicators of depression and real risk factors for mental disease, just as mortality. In view of animal studies and human examinations, the proposed components for these "social buffering" impacts the guideline of stress-related action in the autonomic nervous system (ANS), and hypothalamic-pituitary-adrenal (HPA) gland. Social neuroscience looks into in. People have since a long time ago examined the neurocognitive components by which social help influences physiology and eventually well-being. For instance, in a bunch of studies, social help was found to decrease action in cerebrum locales that are regularly embroiled in the enthusiastic and homeostatic guideline. Specifically, neuro-hemodynamic changes were identified in the front cingulate cortex, dorsolateral and ventrolateral prefrontal cortex and midbrain regions.

The social standard hypothesis (SBT) suggests that life forms are adjusted to social biology—the nearness of different members of the same species.—more so than any physical nature. Thusly, the social nearness to different people (portrayed by nature, joint consideration, shared objectives, and reliance) ought to be considered as the default or standard supposition of the human mind. The base of SBT is the recently done observational investigations that have affirmed that neural pathways and hormonal stress responses identified with self-rule of inclination are less powerful when social assistance is given or even imagined. The neural response to peril sign is restricted when a social associate is accessible. Individuals whose associations are separate by commonality and responsiveness are depicted by reduced self-exertion, which results in a diminished reaction to peril signs.

The SBT is a valuable theory for analyzing singular contrasts in the social baselines of people, specifically with respect to their communication styles. Desire to communicate is an inborn natural framework advancing nearness looking for between a new-born child and a particular connection figure so as to improve the probability of survival, and compassion and connection are reliant. Connection hypothesis offers a convincing stage for understanding a person's ability to interface with others and create steady connections including adapting assets. Studies have exhibited an explicit association between correspondence style and empathy. These detailed researches have demonstrated that individuals with the secure association are progressively open to and understanding others. has been connected with diminished pain constrains. It is said to be a prognostic factor for perpetual pain. It has been additionally demonstrated that unreliable communication may prompt better view of tentatively actuated pain especially within the sight of empathic spectators. All the more, for the most part, communication style directs the advantages of social help, with the end goal that unreliably communicating people report less apparent social help and securely attached people report lower tension levels. Apparently, people that are progressively uncertain in their communications view steady people as less trustworthy, rendering them unfit to involve wholeheartedly in their contacts, and less inclined to profit by social help and empathy.

Trial work has begun to uncover a part of the key neuroanatomical and neurochemical foundations of communication-related techniques and their relationship with other social practices. Such research has clarified different neuropeptides that are unquestionably drawn in with an assortment of association-related social works on including vasopressin, opiates, and oxytocin. It is found that traces of oxytocin can adjust various communication-related practices including trust, empathic concern, and empathic precision. Intranasal oxytocin organization has as of late been appeared to influence cerebral blood perfusion in basic regions in the mind hardware engaged with social discernment and enthusiastic handling, independent of any attending psychological, emotional, or social controls. Critically, oxytocin organization specifically decreases full of feeling responses to compromising social boosts and differentially adjusts visual consideration toward the social sign of positive methodology. In addition, it gives the idea that people lacking amazing social associations show essentially diminished reactions to oxytocin.

In general, there is a developing variety of research demonstrating that emotions give quick, typified data about ebb and flow assets and logical requests, controlling basic leadership by altering the abstract impression of the world. Through the foundation and support of social connections, the assets of social accomplices (guardians, companions, life partners), just as doctors, come to be seen as assets accessible to the person.

Chapter 3: Empath Characteristics, Types and Test

The accompanying rundown of qualities will tell you more about how empaths are.

- **Profoundly sensitive**

Individuals who are normally empathic are exceptionally sensitive to their condition and rapidly since even the smallest changes in others. Their affectability isn't simply restricted to physical sensations – it particularly incorporates relational perspectives. They can "feel into" other individuals and can profoundly comprehend their feelings, inspirations, and emotions.

Exceptionally instinctive

In numerous cases, empaths are profoundly in contact with their own sentiments and feelings. They have a greatly improved understanding of their own emotions than numerous others. Thus, empathic individuals have figured out how to observe their gut impulses and are extremely instinctive. They can detect things sometimes before others observe. Simultaneously, their instinct causes them to evade individuals that are exceptionally dangerous and manipulative.

- **Extremely withdrawn**

You may likewise detest swarmed places, for example, malls, crowded markets, train stations or just such a large number of individuals in the same room. Regularly it's where there is turbulent energy, and the individuals around you are pushed and simply need to get what they are there to do over and finished with.

Because somebody is withdrawn does not really infer they are an empath and the other way around. Not every single empathic individual are essentially self observers. In any case, numerous empaths want to restrain their social cooperations to great lively, kind, and understood companions or relatives. They rapidly feel overpowered when associating with vast gatherings of individuals. Subsequently, they frequently want to invest energy alone, as social cooperations will, in general, enhance their intuitive capacities. An empathic individual explicitly looks for time alone in light of the fact that it encourages them to revive their batteries. One purpose behind this is they can't completely unwind within the sight of other individuals. They can't completely release themselves in these circumstances, which make it unfathomably hard to feel completely calm and agreeable when others are near.

- **Selfless**

Empaths frequently will in general totally overlook their own needs. By and large, they are so worried about the prosperity of others that they thoroughly neglect to deal with themselves. Now and then, empaths may even turn out to be so drenched in a helpful undertaking that they totally dismiss whatever else, regardless of whether it causes them incredible challenges.

- **Associates with others rather quickly**

An empathic individual is capable of connecting with others. Therefore, they can completely comprehend others on a passionate level. Considerably more along these lines, empathic individuals are uncommonly sensitive to how other individuals feel. Because of this extraordinary association with other individuals, empaths are all around prone to assimilate the state of mind and feelings of those they connect with. This intrinsic capacity can make them unknowingly take on a lot of cynicism from others.

Simultaneously, it can happen that they associate way too rapidly with others without taking a note. It could be said, they associate with other individuals on such a private and profound level in such a brief span, that others will most likely be unable to pursue their pace. Thus, these individuals may feel as though the empath is excessively rapidly holding with them, which basically feels unnatural to them.

- **Excessively receptive**

Empaths regularly observe themselves in others. Therefore, they profoundly comprehend the issues and difficulties other individuals are gone up against. Much more in this way, they are very mindful how the psychological weight that a few people carry on their shoulders impacts their conduct. Hence, they are now and then excessively empathetic of other individuals' unsatisfactory and discourteous conduct. Rather than not enabling others to treat them insolently, empaths are in all respects liable to rationalize other individuals' conduct. They are, in a way, magnets to people's emotions.

- **The inclination to put others before themselves**

Individuals that are empathic are not just caring; be that as it may, they likewise tend to put others before themselves. They are normally disposed to accept that the requirements of others are definitely more significant than their own special needs. Empathic individuals are exceptionally caring for others. They are tolerant of other individuals' frailties, shortcomings, and mix-ups. They are regularly ready to see themselves in others, which is the reason they treat others all around benevolent – regardless of whether they don't generally merit it.

- **Finds untruths and duplicities incredibly speedy**

From various perspectives, empaths seem to have one of a kind capacity to rapidly observe through other individuals' untruths and controls. They might be exceptionally suspicious of untruthful individuals, while a large number of their companions haven't seen a thing. Another character characteristic of an empath is that they basically can't stand it to be around dangerous and pompous individuals. They don't just disdain the conduct of these individuals but at the same time are repulsed by the manner in which they treat others.

- **Intrinsic want to better the world**

A considerable lot of the activities of exceptionally empathic individuals are driven by their desire to improve the world. They invest significantly more energy with exercises of a compassionate or magnanimous nature than on progressively conceited undertakings.

- **Curious in nature**

Another character attribute of empaths is their curiosity. They only here and there are happy with the proof that will be found superficially. Consequently, they persistently attempt to perceive what is taken cover behind the window ornament. Also, they over and over again ask about the idea of the real world. Not exclusively are they continually looking for answers yet they likewise love to suggest themselves provocative conversation starters that cause them to philosophize.

- **Inattentiveness**

Empaths are frequently seen to be preoccupied, distracted, or oblivious. In practically all examples, empathic individuals are so overpowered by the ocean of feelings they are swimming in, that they thoroughly lose their ground. They are influenced by the confused feelings they are encompassed with, which regularly drives them to turn out to be completely submerged in this contemplation and feelings.

- **Ability to acknowledge full duty**

Various individuals are stood up to with the issue that they constantly reprimand others for their own deficiencies. An empathic individual is a remarkable inverse. Rather than routinely looking for the deficiency in their condition or outer conditions, empaths assume full responsibility for their very own activities. In numerous occurrences, this enormously causes them to impact helpful changes in their lives. In any case, it can likewise happen that they acknowledge duty regarding things they are not in any manner in charge of.

- **Profoundly imaginative**

An empathic individual is imaginative. They want to invest their energy with exercises that enable them to utilize their creative mind and inventiveness. Empaths are bound to be craftsmen, scholars, performers, painters, and planners than bookkeepers, legal advisors, and specialists.

- **Effectively diverted, the propensity to wander off in fantasy land**

Empaths battle to stay in reality, particularly when connecting with numerous individuals or when performing undertakings they despise. These two circumstances frequently lead them to turn out to be completely inundated in their own thoughts.

- **The propensity to invest much energy alone**

To an empathic individual, communicating with individuals can be – both rationally and physically – depleting. This is particularly evident when they are gone up against insensible, little disapproved, and narrow-minded individuals. Consequently, empaths are all around liable to plan some "alone time" so as to revive their drained batteries. In any case, if empathic individuals can't invest energy with themselves, they rapidly experience passionate over-burden.

- **Regularly fixated on keeping things spick and span**

On the off chance that there's one thing empathic individuals completely don't care for it is disarray and mess. Consequently, they incline toward moderate and mess-free conditions. In numerous examples, they themselves are minimalists.

- **Trouble to distinguish the wellspring of feelings**

At the point when an empathic individual is interacting with others, they may regularly struggle to separate between other individuals' feelings and their own. Subsequently, they are not constantly ready to distinguish if certain feelings they experience to begin from inside themselves or not.

- **Frequently abused as a dumping ground for psychological weight**

Empaths frequently comprehend the enthusiastic scene of another person much superior to anything the individual themselves does. Subsequently, a large number of their companions will look for an interview and help during times of incredible challenges. Lamentably, a few people abuse empaths just to dispose of their psychological weight without really thinking about the empathic individual.

- **Experiences exhaustion**

Numerous empaths continually feel depleted without truly knowing why. This can form into an extremely serious issue, particularly when the individual being referred to doesn't know about their high reasonableness towards other individuals' feelings. Fortunately, numerous empathic individuals gradually start to comprehend that investing energy alone encourages them to energize their batteries after social connections. This, thusly, encourages them to diminish the weakness they experience.

- **Aversion of savagery and dramatization**

It's nothing unexpected that one never goes over an empath that appreciates observing any type of savagery on TV. They are, by and large, truly hopeful individuals, which is the reason they are not especially enamored with watching or perusing dread based news reports. Additionally, they don't prefer to take part in merciless or vicious extra time exercises.

- **Unequivocally associated with animals**

Another extremely fascinating quality of empathic individuals is that they can associate more profoundly with animals than general others. They connect with animals without any effort. In a way, they communicate naturally. Most of them are animal lovers and enjoy connecting with animals' emotions.

- **They can't say "no"**

Empathic individuals staggeringly struggle in circumstances where they need to dismiss others. By and large, they don't generally prefer to say "no." actually, they will regularly give their absolute best to keep away from such circumstances. The explanation behind this is very straightforward: they profoundly see how harmful it is to be rejected. They likewise know instinctively how terrible a "no" can be, particularly when one actually needs assistance. Subsequently, empathic individuals regularly acknowledge duties without thinking about their very own restrictions.

- **Issues with digestion**

Try not to ask for what valid reason this is the situation, however, strangely enough, numerous empaths have stomach related issue. One explanation behind this could be that empaths, for the most part, have fiery issues in the territory where the sun oriented plexus is found.

- **Overpowered when connections get excessively private**

As was at that point referenced in the above mentioned, numerous empaths need much time for themselves. Be that as it may, when they are in a cozy relationship, time alone can be very rare. Subsequently, numerous empathic individuals feel extraordinarily overpowered with connections that get excessively personal. To them, such a relationship imperils their capacity to revive drained batteries. Simultaneously, they might fear to lose themselves and their character in the relationship.

- **Facelower back issues**

It was at that point tended to that numerous empathic individuals experience the ill effects of stomach related issues. Another result of vivacious issues in the sunlight based plexus zone can show as lower back issues. Different sources describe these issues to the way that an individual that does not realize that they are an empath, so they are less inclined to take part in exercises that ground them.

- **Completely abhor unfair treatment in all aspects**

Empathic individuals just can't stand it to be gone up against with treacheries. To them, it doesn't make a difference whether they are influenced by it or not. They are frequently totally overpowered by the foul play they themselves and other individuals are encountering. Such shameful acts to give them a hugely extreme time as well as motivation empaths to look for potential arrangements, regardless of whether this hunt takes weeks or months.

- **Like to help unfortunate people**

An empath feels attracted to dark horses and will regularly give their absolute best to help them in any capacity they can.

- **Free-lively**

Elevated amounts of control, rules, and tight guidelines are soul-pulverizing according to an empath. Also, complying with such principles and being compelled to adjust to fixed schedules feels profoundly detaining to an empath. While numerous others have a sense of safety in such stable conditions, empathic individuals incline toward opportunity, independence, and experience. They just love to be independent.

- **Especially focused on genuinely feeble individuals**

Empaths are always targeted by individuals who – either intentionally or unknowingly – try to deplete their energy. The impact of these vampires frequently leaves empathic individuals feeling drained, depleted, and mysteriously discouraged. These sincerely frail individuals are, for example, narcissists, dramatization rulers, self-saw exploited people, and numerous other damaging individuals.

- **Headed to invest energy in nature**

Nature encourages empathic individuals to revive. They may some way or another vibe calmer and revived when being in nature. Investing energy outside causes them to ground themselves and to discharge the weight of a chaotic and occupied condition.

- **Regularly went up against with synchronicities**

It regularly appears as though empathic individuals are more tuned in to themselves as well as other people. Therefore, they frequently experience unexplainable synchronicities. They might consider a specific individual just minutes before this for an individual calls them on the telephone. Or on the other hand, they may feel that a darling individual is by one way or another in a tough situation, regardless of whether that individual is far away.

- **Effectively controlled by others**

In the abovementioned, we've officially secured that empaths have attempted to state "no." Consequently, they are regularly gone up against individuals that have figured out how to control them by utilizing remorseful fits. These controllers have found that the empathic individual battles to meet choices that make others feel baffled or irate, which is the reason they can without much of a stretch adventure them.

- **As a rule excessively liberal in viewpoints and lifestyle**

On the off chance that one of your companions is a profoundly empathic individual, you will realize that their generosity and enormous heartedness (nearly) knows no restrictions. Empathic individuals care, as it were, for the prosperity of others. In many cases, they attempt to tackle other individuals' issues and to assuage their misery. In numerous occasions, nonetheless, empaths give so liberally that they are either misused or essentially don't have the foggiest idea when they have arrived at their restrictions.

- **Finely-tuned faculties**

Another significant normal for practically all empaths is the way that their faculties are profoundly tuned. For some others, such an individual may show up as excessively sensitive.

- **Secret confidante to huge numbers of their companions**

Without truly knowing why, numerous empaths are the picked associates of their companions, relatives, and those they connect with. They regularly hear sentences, for example, "I've never told this anybody" or "I don't realize for what reason am disclosing to you this." by and large, numerous individuals feel truly good around empaths and are hence bound to share personal privileged insights that they wouldn't impart to any other individual.

Other than the characteristics mentioned above, you can always check out if you are an empath.

- You might be sensitive to loud noises. They may not be disturbing, however, they have an inclination that they affect you directly. You are sensitive to harsh lights, strong scents. The energy of these things can really initiate a state where you are encountering negative sentiments activated by them.

- You may encounter times of nervousness for no obvious reason. Regardless of what you do, you can't release it or get over it, and you have no clue why.

- You are clinically discouraged or feel discouraged for no evident reason. By and by, regardless of what you attempt, you can't 'get over it'.

- You take a great deal of blame, regardless of whether it's for another's activity or for something you have done that has been gotten in a manner you didn't expect or want.

- You feel overly sensitive to individuals whether there is a need to associate with you or not. In reality, in the event that you sense that you are not invited at someplace or by somebody willingly but the other person is not conveying it, you will quickly take the nearest exit which you can find.

- You feel ungrounded. That is, you are all in your psyche, as opposed to your body. When you are someplace where you don't feel great or are exhausted, or simply don't wish to be there, you will frequently withdraw into your creative mind, and travel to far away and inaccessible spots. This kind of not-being-rooted feeling is highly disturbing to an empath as they derive their energy from natural elements. Being among people may drain them of their empath abilities.

- You can generally tell how another person feels, regardless of whether they reveal to you something different. This is frequently taken actually, however, by and large, it's simply the other individual having issues, which have nothing to do with you. The closer you are to somebody, the more you will fear it has to do with you.

- You will, in general, assume the best about individuals. You ensure that somebody has been given every opportunity, and that's only the tip of the iceberg before you act to prevent them from accomplishing something that might damage or putting you under strain. Regardless of whether this individual is acting like a total jerk, despite everything you will attempt to give them understanding and empathy. Tragically, in this present world, doing such things is regularly mishandled, or worse, you end up being the terrible individual.

- You feel an extraordinary association with creatures and things of nature, including plants and trees. In fact, you may detect the vitality of a zone in all respects empathically, be it positive or negative.

- If you see somebody in trouble, pain or who are suffering, you will naturally feel inclined to them, so as to make them feel that they are not the only one. You may even feel their physical pain and unquestionably feel their emotional distress. You may really feel regretful in the event that you don't understand such an individual and will regularly set aside your own needs, regardless of whether you happen to feel better. You can't stand another's anguish.

- You may want to help, recuperate and spare others from themselves. It is significant for the empath to not bounce directly in an attempt to 'fix' somebody who they see to experience an unpleasant time. This is a snare numerous empaths can fall into, however frequently their assistance isn't constantly welcomed, or is mishandled, and the empath winds up being utilized and depleted of crucial energy and assets. An empath has a method for recognizing on the off chance that they ought to support somebody or not.

- You have an inbuilt untruth finder. Somebody can be revealing to you a flagrant deception; however, you will know whether it's not valid. The intriguing thing about this is you may not know immediately, however you will know, and soon. Individuals will frequently attempt to trick you; however once you have had the opportunity to strengthen each one of those sentiments, you will consistently know whether somebody is attempting to deceive you or control you.

- Many empaths are common healers and can recuperate others either with the laying of hands or from a separation.

Empaths are commonly attracted to healing others or a calling that guides others somehow or another.

- If somebody discovers something entertaining or dismal or has a solid assessment about a specific subject, you may end up connecting with them, so as to coordinate their energies. At that point, you may end up doing it with the following individual who tags along. You generally wind up in concurrence with who you are with and you possibly feel your actual emotions when you are along. This doesn't mean you are indecisive or powerless, it implies that you are checking out who the individual is and what they are feeling, and enabling their energies to overpower yours. Numerous empaths do this since they feel it will help construct an affinity with the other, yet all it truly does is discredit what your identity is, and nobody expresses gratitude toward you for it either. Remaining in your very own space and power can be very tiring for an empath.

- You do not feel like you have a place with this world. Surely, the empath will regularly feel like a fish out of water, and genuinely accept that they do not have a place here. That is on the grounds that the conduct of others is so odd and an outsider to them, they can't relate.

- You may feel overpowered by such a large number of individuals, energies or feelings happening at the same time. Being an empath resembles being a clairvoyant sponge. On the off chance that you do not have command over your capacities, and ability to cleanse, you will, in the long run, go into harmful over-burden, particularly when there is so much clairvoyant contamination out there. In some cases having a purging, shower can do some amazing things.

- You and others see yourself as an exceptionally touchy individual. Indeed, even the littlest change in dispositions can be grabbed by you. It very well may be extremely perplexing.

- While somebody might be an empath, it doesn't restrict them to simply being an empath. They may likewise have or create other mystic capacities, for example, clairvoyance, directing, special insight, and so forth. Sympathy is one part of our mystic capacities.

- There is no disgrace in being an empath. You ought not to need to conceal this from others, or even yourself. What your identity is a gift, and you can possibly improve other individuals' lives so much that they will rush to associate with you. The empath can get feelings, yet they can likewise send, and where they feel torment in others, they can, rather than taking on the agony, send happiness and recuperating. You can truly bring somebody out from their most profound sadness just by doing this, and being you.

- If you feel that you fit a portion of the qualities, or even every one of them, at that point truly, you are an empath.

- When you show profound compassion toward others, their protective energy goes down, and positive vitality replaces it. That is the point at which you can get progressively inventive in taking care of issues.

EMPATH TEST

After going through the empath characteristics, you might have a lot of questions. There must be so many questions in your mind about you being an empath. On the off chance that you identified the majority of above-mentioned characteristics, here is your chance to quickly take an empath test which will affirm your beliefs. This empath test is a short version. If you say "yes" to these inquiries you might be an empath.

Everyone has empathy in lesser or greater degree but only a few are empaths at heart. Of course, if you are curious about your empathic nature, this

This test scores you on a few classifications, including regardless of whether you are an out of control healer, how well you utilize your own empathic protection tools, the amount of empathy you unconsciously mirror to other individuals, and how logical versus intuitive you are.

To decide how empathic you are, take the accompanying self-evaluation test.

1. Do people think that I am overly touchy or humble?

2. Do I oftentimes get overwhelmed by different sensations and feel on-edge?

3. Do I hate loud noises and they make me feel sick?

4. Do I feel different from others?

5. Do I constantly become overwhelmed when in-crowd and find a way out when I feel trapped?

6. Does commotion, scents, or constant talkers make me feel uneasy and repulsed?

7. Do I feel overly sensitive to strong scents or too tight clothes which constantly rub on my skin?

8. Do I always need my vehicle around myself so I can escape when I want to?

9. Do I indulge to adapt to pressure?

10. Am I terrified of getting to be choked by personal connections?

11. Is it easy to make me scared?

12. Do caffeine or drugs affect me a lot?

13. Do I have a low threshold for pain?

14. Do I avoid people in general?

15. Do I retain other individuals' feelings or stress?

16. Do I feel crumble under pressure by multiple tasks?

17. Do I feel relieved in natural surroundings?

18. Do I need quite a while to recover in the wake of being with troublesome individuals or vitality vampires?

19. Improve in little urban areas or the nation than huge urban areas?

20. Do I lean toward coordinated collaborations or little bunches instead of

On the off chance that you addressed yes to one to five inquiries, you're at any rate somewhat an empath.

If you said yes to 6 to 10 of the questions implies, there are good chances that you are a moderate empath.

If you answered yes to 11 to 15 questions, it means you have dense empathic inclinations.

If you answered yes to more than 15 questions, you are undoubtedly an empath.

Empath Types

Like other things, even empaths have types. Have a look at them to know more about your empathic abilities.

Emotional empath

This is the class regularly partner with empaths. Emotional empaths are known for detecting and feeling the feelings of others. They will see through any façade or front that someone else might set up to shroud how they are truly feeling. Not at all like other empathic or exceptionally delicate individuals, have enthusiastic

Empaths really experienced the feelings that other individuals are feeling.

Restorative empath

Restorative empaths will feel or realize other individuals' hurts, agonies, and ailments. This might be instinctive mindfulness or a feeling of what indications another person has. They may feel the equivalent physical manifestations or torment in their own body. The pressure, agony, sensation, and feelings of others' ailments can be washed over them and effectively showed through the empath's body. They additionally frequently sense what the other individual may require regarding mending and this leads them to be gifted healers.

Animal empath

An animal empath can tune into the sentiments and thoughts of other creature life around them to a degree that they can collaborate and empathically impact the creature's behavior. These empaths know what a creature is feeling, facing and needs. They feel a more profound shared connection with almost all animal species.

Nature empath

Nature empaths are people who can communicate with nature and needs of plants and trees. They are plant specialists and cultivators who love being in nature. They can hear the thoughts of the plants, which enables them to be exceptionally talented plant specialists, as they can tune into what the plants they work with require to flourish. These empaths likewise feel a deep connection with the earth. During natural disasters, nature empaths regularly experience negative energy.

Scholarly empath

Scholarly Empaths see how the mind functions and can undoubtedly get a handle on another person's point of view. They want to learn and keep on examining an assortment of subjects for the duration of their lives. These Empaths can change their correspondence style in a split second to coordinate any discussion they are having.

Precognitive empath

Precognitive empaths experience dreams about future occasions. They may encounter these as a hunch, feeling, or as a clear dream.

Psychometric empath

Psychometric empaths perceive the energy in lifeless things including apparel, photos, souvenirs, and adornments.

Precious stone empath

Precious stone empaths feel a ground-breaking association with gems and utilize these for information, motivation, and profound investigation.

Clairvoyant empath

Clairvoyant empaths are regularly considered "personality perusers" since they can encounter someone else's unexpressed thoughts.

Mechanical empath

A mechanical Empath intrinsically gets machines. They can detect what is important to fix a machine, even without specialized learning.

Astral empath

Astral empaths can straightforwardly connect with astral creatures, including angels, pixies, heavenly attendants, or ETs.

Law enforcement empath

Law Enforcement empaths share the uncommon capacity to fathom wrongdoings and find missing people.

Atomic empath

Atomic empaths experience others at the sub-atomic level, which gives them a profound comprehension of an individual's quintessence. This capacity is useful for healing and instructing.

Geomantic empath

Geomantic Empaths feel the vitality left in a particular spot. They can stroll into a room and realize that a noteworthy contention occurred there only hours sooner. These Empaths are regularly attracted to investigate cemeteries, places of worship or old houses for reasons unknown. Certain spots can trigger forceful feelings and the Geomantic Empath might be attracted to an area or feel a solid direness to leave.

Spiritual empath

Such empaths have astuteness about someone else's association with the divine powers. They see profoundly the relationship other individuals have to a higher power.

Claircognizant empath

Claircognizant empaths can see past non-verbal communication, outward appearances and words to comprehend someone else's profound mysteries. They can detect an individual's genuine emotions, paying little heed to what that individual is stating.

Medium empath

Medium empaths have a setup association with the heavenly world. They can interface with the spirits of the deceased. These empaths can encounter the emotions, thoughts, and mental impressions of divine creatures.

How Empathy Works for Empaths

While there is much we don't yet comprehend how empathy functions, we do have some information. Everything has an energetic vibration or recurrence and an empath can detect these vibrations and perceive even the subtlest changes imperceptible to the unaided eye.

Expressions of articulation hold a lively design that starts with the speaker. They have particular importance specific to the speaker. Behind that articulation is a power or power field, otherwise called energy. For instance, the feeling of hate frequently achieves an extraordinary inclination that promptly goes with the word. The word hate gets escalated with the speaker's feelings. It is that individual's sentiments (vitality) that are gotten by empaths, regardless of whether the words are verbally expressed, thought or just felt without verbal or real articulation.

Psychic empathic qualities include the capacity to receive energy, yet in addition, incorporate the capacity to heal much of the time. Therefore, an empath's life way is most appropriate to the healing expressions, regardless of whether it is in the field of human services or guiding, or working with children, plants, animals, or notwithstanding healing spots through structure and redesign. There is a wide range of ways for how to turn into an empathic energy healer - you simply need to figure out which attributes and levels of an empath impact you most. When you have a constructive option for the mystic capacities of being empathic, you can encounter harmony and satisfaction. This enables you to conquer the staggering sentiments of why an empath feels the tension.

Meditation can be useful for anybody to accomplish a condition of harmony, yet what is significantly increasingly significant for those with mystic empathic
qualities are to keep up steady grounding and assurance. You should envision yourself encompassed by an air pocket or cover of white light that shields and shields you from outside energies. On the off chance that you are a highly sensitive one, you might need

to build these limits of security by envisioning a rainbow of layers around yourself, beginning with an air pocket of encompassing your body, trailed by a layer of orange light, at that point yellow around that, at that point green, at that point blue, at that point indigo, at that point a layer of violet light, lastly a layer of white light around them all. It is likewise imperative to imagine yourself grounded and associated with the Earth so you can stay adjusted, steady and secure.

It is useful to utilize the phrase "I will get all that is for the most astounding and best for me to know, and I am shielded and protected from all else consistently." For empaths, it is essential to protect themselves from the negative energies of others (narcissists).

Keep in mind that those with mystic empathic characteristics are not just ready to receive and absorb the energy of others; they can likewise emit healing vibrations as well. The reason that empaths receive energy and information, in any case, is on the grounds that they have the ability to take care of others.

What an Empath Feels

Perhaps the most effortless strategy for how to turn into an empathic vitality healer is just by utilizing your aim. When you get emotions from others, or even from the entire world, you can invert the extremity and convey healing energy. Close your eyes, envision that there is a huge sun above you that is sending down a light emission into your heart and down into your hands. With the majority of your will and aim, send that light out from your heart and your hands, and direct it to any place it needs to go for the most elevated and best great of all.

This is the thing that will give you harmony. What's to come isn't unchangeable and we are not unfortunate casualties. We have an endowment of freedom and the ability to change, so we should not be apprehensive, notwithstanding when it appears to be overpowering.

Empaths have unstructured energy zones. They move their energy fields in and around the energy fields of other individuals so as to look at how they are feeling. They do this naturally so as to realize how to get what they need, so as to be sheltered, or so as to comprehend what is around them. As they develop more established a few people learn different strategies for protection, seeing verbally, or techniques for getting data. A few people don't learn different techniques and keep on being empathic, sponge-like in absorbing energy, information, and feelings from other individuals. These individuals think that it's extremely hard to comprehend where they stop and someone else starts. They tend to enable their limits to be attacked by other individuals. They don't comprehend the idea of individual limits. At the point when an individual is empathic, it is hard for them to have a decent mental self-view that isn't constrained by the musings of other individuals about them. They don't have an unmistakable impression of selfhood and "others." This endowment of having the option to peruse other individuals empathically turns out to be to a greater extent a curse rather than a blessing. Thus, it is important that empaths learn to protect themselves from the negative influences of people.

It is an opportunity to quit any pretense of being empathic and to rather get information for and about other individuals by conversing straightforwardly with their soul. In being empathic they are getting information from others and conveying it for them or acting it out for them, unknowingly. It is hard to separate between what are our sentiments and feelings and the feelings of others. Being empathic makes numerous individuals be stressed and to be exorbitantly emotional. They can stop to work on being unwittingly empathic by introducing purposeful inflatables of protective energy around ourselves, and by having an expectation to convey clairvoyantly (as opposed to an empathically) with the souls of those we experience. Trust just your very own instinct. Trust just what resounds with your very own reality.

Chapter 4: Empathy in Different Life Zones

Empathy is the capacity to experience and identify with the musings, feelings or experiences of others. It is the capacity to venture into another person's shoes, know about their sentiments and comprehend their needs. But how is it relevant to our lives? It is. We need empathy in our life experiences, and this is essential to maintain the collective conscience of humanity. Be it workplace, relationships, sex, friendships, and/or strangers; empathy is lacking in all of these life segments. Having a look at empathy's role is crucial. The main problem is that stress has been so normalized that tensions, feuds, and everything negative are considered normal. What's worse? If you are an empath who is in stressful and pressured situations, you might end up being exploited. But it can be a good thing too. Let's have a look at empathy's role in different scenarios to understand better.

It is generally agreed upon that empathy is something worth being thankful for, and that it should be the premise of frames of mind towards patient care, or ought to, at any rate, assume a significant job in the patient-doctor relationship which includes physical assessments, and treatment. Increasingly more frequently, therapeutic instruction highlights the importance of empathy in the medicinal field, and a developing number of medical schools have started instructing their understudies about the importance of being empathic with the patients. Quite recently, an abundance of studies and research has inspected the empathy from various viewpoints. Be that as it may, the vast majority of this scholarly research has concentrated on the empathizer.

Empathy certainly has found a way to intrigue the researchers. This will lead the way to more research in this field.

Importance of Empathy at Medical Establishments

Regardless of the variety that portrays the idea of empathy, this idea is generally utilized in patient-centric practices and progressively unmistakable in contemporary healing techniques. A few theorists contend that empathy is neither fundamental nor adequate to ensure great medication. While empathy has consistently been viewed as a fundamental segment of empathy-based patient care, there has been a significant research on the significance of empathy in medical field, how it can be utilized properly, and how it can be enhanced in medical practitioners' daily behavior when they are at work tending to people they don't know.

Such studies and researches have led to the flood of intrigue and excitement in the idea which is about contemplating empathic patient-doctor relations. In psychiatry and clinical psychology, an empathic mental state enables the practitioner to communicate and garner essential data about the patient. It also adds to building a dependable, reliable relationship between the patient and caretaker. Empathy is likewise a significant component of value human services in the medical field. Doctors who endeavor to comprehend what their patients are feeling, regardless of empathic precision or just truly imparting their empathic concern, accomplish various important results for their patients. On the other hand, it could just be truly imparting empathic concern which can result in churning out various important results. For instance, a specialist's mindful contact instead of an analytic touch is seen as passing on clinical empathy and advances healing.

All the more important in the healing fields, tolerant impression of doctor's empathy is related to improved well-being results. Patients give more full narratives to those medical practitioners sensitive to them without telling it. Empathic care is shown to improve patient satisfaction, better adherence to treatment, and fewer cases of medical negligence. It goes the same way for better wellbeing, prosperity, and expert fulfillment of doctors.

Critically, intellectual empathy can improve understanding of fulfillment. One of the most important aspects of empathy goes a long way than anyone can imagine.

Empathic concern is essential to patient adherence to treatment schedules, with a beneficial connection between patient-doctor empathy and expanded fulfillment and consistency to treatment. Patients tend to respond better to those doctors who do not treat them merely as subjects but as humans. Rude doctors tend to have stressed outpatients which may affect the recovery rate. Even if witnessed in real settings by a layman, this thing is shown to be true and impactful.

In medicine, empathy has significant ramifications for the patient's well-being results, and also in addition to doctor achievement. Specialists who show empathy commit less negligence and a better understanding of fulfillment and consistency. One research revealed that while there is much irregularity in regards with the impact of psychological consideration, doctors who receive a warm, benevolent, and consoling way are considered more trustworthy than the individuals who keep meetings formal and don't offer consolation. Care based intercessions that upgrade consideration, mindfulness, and relational abilities, increase compassion and improve the doctor's prosperity and mental health as well.

What Problems Healthcare Providers Can Face?

Empathy has limits for medical practitioners as well. We need the specialist to see how we feel, yet we don't really need them to cry when we cry, and we surely need them to stay cool in crises. What's more, such are the circumstances human services experts need to go up against once a day – pain, stress, and death– that not many could get by without a level of expert detachment. These mental weights of care can be a central point in staff 'burnout', which can make it harder to be compassionate. Yes, a line has to be drawn.

It is critical to take note of that being too empathic can be stressful for medical professionals. In any case, a tiny level of individual stress (or emotional sharing/attunement), is essential for the doctors' proficient personal satisfaction. Since doctors are presented to large amounts of negative feelings in unpleasant situations, they can develop empathy weakness and serious emotional depletion, which may desensitize them and increase the danger of medical blunders. Studies and neuroscience research shows that people who can direct their very own full of feeling reactions to keep up an ideal degree of emotional excitement have more prominent articulations of empathic worry for other people

By and large, there is a strong and collective proof that all features of empathy assume a significant job in therapeutic practice and affect both the patient and doctor. Empathy at medical settings can improve the patient's mental as well as physical well-being especially after recovering from an illness, add to recuperating, and can influence the general prosperity of the beneficiary; a reality that requires an unthinking clarification.

Empathy at the workplace

Social collaboration in our work environments is progressively significant as robotization replaces basic assignments, pushing our employees and employers into more learning-based and the board jobs. The functional economy depends on social communication and societies that advance and encourage these connections. At present, we are seeing a reduction in empathy and increment in narcissism, especially in our young people. Empathy, the capacity to comprehend and share the sentiments of another, encourages correspondence, assembles trust, and debilitates hostility and tormenting. It is a basic fixing in positive authoritative societies that are social capital.

Such huge numbers of our representatives are presently immune to empathy. Those who have less empathy are celebrated as dedicated workers. Sociopath tendencies are increasing as a result. Since sociopathy is a continuum of seriousness we essentially mean somebody who has some trouble understanding or sharing someone else's emotions. For instance, we all have experienced bosses who refuse to listen to employees and expect them to work like machines. One single day of problem and the chances of getting fired increase. This pattern of lessening in compassion and increment in narcissism has been credited to the ascent of technology-dependent workplaces. It's most likely settled in parts of current culture, for example, intensity and fundamental dread of not succeeding, the rat race to earn riches, massive pay disparity, voyeurism, and fear.

Indeed, technology-based life empowers self-advancement and the chase to be successful that outcomes in narcissism. Having little regard for others is so normal that an emotional person is not seen as a perfect fit to be an employee. Even if an empath ends up in a company, the consistent presentation to issues and stressful occasions can prompt empathy exhaustion and affirmation predisposition that adds to a relative passionate separate from others. At the same time, individuals collaborating through innovation miss the meaningful gestures related to close and personal communication, lessening their capability to peruse and decipher these signs. These signals are crucial to sympathy so it's sensible that an absence of capacity to comprehend expressive gestures will bring about diminished compassion. Remember, an empath's only weakness is to not being able to draw a line. Most of the empathic employees end up being exploited as they understand and the pressure their boss is facing from superiors.

This is especially critical for young adults who are as yet learning and discovering their place in the public arena. Youngsters and grown-ups who invest energy in the technology-infiltrated life are passing up close and personal cooperations that would enable them to learn meaningful gestures and create sympathy. It is anything but an act of futility. We need to battle the tide of the more extensive cultural culture; however, we can make our way of life inside our association or gathering. Furthermore, that is a battle worth battling.

What can be done?

To changing degrees relying upon the person, when individuals enter another circumstance they glance around for prompts to how they should act. They look for data about how things work in our association or gathering, how they should act and even think. Whether you are a boss or not, you can still initiate change. To encourage a more profound comprehension of the significance of sympathy in the work environment, we need to understand how empathy contributes to the workplace.

Empathy is a learned trait. A great many people who score high on appraisals for compassion have no clue why; maybe they are raised that way or they have seen things spiraling out of control, and they lend an ear or shoulder for another person to lean upon. They don't comprehend what it is they do that makes others consider them to be empathic. They can just express that they like individuals, appreciate working with and helping other people, and consider individuals as people worthy of compassion. Empaths might never notice their inner compassion, but they are useful elements who make things better for everyone. Some draw a line, some don't. Yet one can never dismiss the importance of empathy.

For instance, show others how empathy can be a useful tool. Show compassion towards everybody in your association or group. Urge others to demonstrate compassion and discover approaches to recognize the individuals who do. An act of kindness and understanding never goes waste. Lending an ear to listen to another person at the workplace will only be beneficial. This is especially true for new joiners, who are finding out about the new, very different way of life than their previous company. Making them feel comfortable is the first step to gain trust. At first, their faculties will strain for any proof of "how it is," however as they settle in they will develop trust in the company's way of life.

You have to guarantee clear messages are sent from the earliest starting point and nothing repudiates the way of life you need to make. We might utilize compassion tested individuals yet we can't think little of the job of working environment culture in making increasingly sympathetic activities in our association. In the working environment, compassion can demonstrate profound regard for associates and demonstrate that you give it a second thought, rather than simply passing by standards and guidelines. An empathic initiative style can make everybody feel like a group and increment profitability, resolve and faithfulness. Compassion is an integral asset in the initiative belt of a well-enjoyed and regarded official.

We could all take an exercise from medical attendants about being sympathetic. On numerous occasions, medical attendants rate as the most reliable in calling. Since they utilize legitimate compassion to make patients feel thought about and safe. Stress is there too, but their main job is to make the patient comfortable. And most of them do know the right things to say to put other people at ease.

Most of the people do it without making much effort.

By understanding others we grow nearer connections. The radar of each great official just went off when they read "connections." This is not an awful thing since a great many people comprehend the issues that happen when inappropriate connections are created in the working environment. All together for a group of employees and their pioneers to work intensely together, legitimate connections must be manufactured and extended. A fist is stronger than individual fingers and empathy is the glue which binds all together with mutual understanding, care and respect. At the point when this occurs through empathy, trust is ingrained in the group. At the point when trust is assembled, beneficial things start to occur.

Empathy requires three things: tuning in, receptiveness and comprehension.

Compassionate individuals listen mindfully to what you're letting them know, placing their total spotlight on the individual before them and not getting effectively diverted. They invest more energy tuning in than talking since they need to comprehend the challenges others face, all of which gives everyone around them the sentiment of being heard and perceived.

Compassionate officials and administrators understand that the reality of any business is just come through and with individuals. Accordingly, they have a frame of mind of receptiveness towards and comprehension of the sentiments and feelings of their colleagues.

Let us put it this way; when we understand our group, we have a superior thought of the difficulties in front of us. Empathy enables us to have a sense of security with our disappointments since we won't just be accused of them. If we talk about getting late to work, it is considered as one of the main things an employee dreads. As explained earlier, having the position of "boss" should not stop one from being an empath. Even if an employee is late,
empathy urges the authority figure to comprehend the main driver behind terrible showing without compromising with the office work. Being compassionate enables pioneers to help battling representatives improve and exceed expectations. Having a narcissist boss or colleague is a nightmare for a lot of us. So, why an act of compassion isn't being taken when the benefits are immense?

Empathy assumes a noteworthy job in the working environment for each association that will manage disappointments, terrible performance, and representatives who need to succeed. The job of a boss (and even an employee) is straightforward—manage the group, be empathic and watches them create a solid and prosperous association.

However, the main problem is that despite knowing about the benefits of empathy, we aren't being progressively compassionate at work. Why? Because one needs to take a step forward to move ahead. If the boss is super strict and considers that empathy is a weakness, they need to realize the benefits it would do to others, and them. As an empathic employee, you can be supportive, understanding and encouraging while taking a step back to recharge yourself. Sympathy takes work. Exhibiting empathy requires some investment and exertion to indicate mindfulness and comprehension. It's not in every case straightforward why a worker thinks or feels how they do about a circumstance. It also means putting others in front of yourself, which can be a test in the present focused working environment. Numerous associations are centered on accomplishing objectives regardless of the expense to representatives.

While the pressure is immense a yelling boss or an uncooperative colleague will never be appreciated. What recognizes normal to average pioneers from the individuals who exceed expectations?

The differentiation gets through the capacity of the pioneer who effectively neutralizes all the supposed "reasons" and consolidates a frame of mind of sympathy all through their association. That sort of pioneer will exceed expectations.

By investing more energy finding out about the requirements of their workers, bosses, leaders, and employees can establish the pace and approach taken by their representatives to accomplish their company's objectives.

This is a reality that has long stood the trial of time. It is valid for our connections all through the working environment.

EMPATHY IN ROMANTIC RELATIONSHIPS

can Empathy is the core of the relationship and there is no doubt in that. Without it, the relationship will find it hard to survive long-term. That's since sympathy requires empathy. Also, without sympathy, couples can't build up a bond. This is a bond which needs a strong glue of love to survive.

The significance of empathy for a romantic relationship is that it bridges the partition between being independent people with various foundations, sentiments, and viewpoints.

Empathy combined with love is a strong mix of transparency and warmth, which enables us to reach, to take get a kick out of and acknowledge, to be at one with ourselves, others, and life itself.

Without empathy, we can't reach the couple goals.

To have a sound, solid relationship, it's significant for you and your accomplice to feel profoundly associated with one another. While it might be simpler to keep up this during the special first-night stage, being powerless in your relationship and observing approaches to be progressively sympathetic to your accomplice can help with fortifying that passionate bond.

Being empathic you are mindful of your better half's feelings and can see from their point of view; you feel what they feel, you get hurt when they get hurt. In spite of the fact that it's essential to be empathic in each domestic relationship you have, it's fundamental to keep up strong love and empathy for each other. Regardless of to what extent you've been with your partner, feeling comprehended and heard is an extraordinary method to feel like you and your accomplice are tied together strongly with the strings of love. Be that as it may, to totally comprehend being empathic, it's great to know the distinction from simply being thoughtful. Empathy drives association and strengthen a marriage.

For what reason is an absence of compassion an issue for a marriage or a close relationship?

An absence of empathy is one of the characterizing attributes of low emotional quotient.

You should be happy to step outside of your own needs and sentiments so as to be available and drawn in with another person.

Empathy calls for persistence, undivided attention, closeness, and magnanimity. It requires a liberal and giving soul and a genuine want to sit with somebody in their most troublesome minutes or offer in their most blissful achievements.

A few people are normally compassionate, yet individuals who need empathy can learn and strengthen their abilities by making an effort.

To do that, we should perceive its worth in our connections, yet additionally in our very own development. Rehearsing compassion extends our comprehension of ourselves as well as other people.

It interfaces us to the human condition. The anguish, the delights, the distresses, and the longings both partners share as a whole. It attracts us closer to the individuals around us and liberates us to be powerless and genuine with them.

We have to rehearse empathy in the majority of our own and expert connections, yet the one relationship wherein compassion is fundamental are your marriage or love relationship.

Empathy causes you to settle struggle and mistaken assumptions, as you are additionally ready to see your accomplice's point of view and comprehend their emotions. It gives you knowledge into the most profound openings of your accomplice's passionate world, permitting you a fuller encounter of the individual you are hitched to. Not only that, empathy demonstrates your partner that you cherish them enough to be completely drawn in love with each other.

An absence of empathy makes you have less sensitive and be increasingly judgmental with other individuals throughout your life. You start focusing more on yourself while completely neglecting your partner.

Self-ingestion in the entirety of its structures kills sympathy, not to mention empathy. When we center on ourselves, our reality contracts as our issues and distractions pose a potential threat. In any case, when we center on others, our reality grows. Our own issues float to the fringe of the brain thus appear to be trivial, and we attempt to increase our ability for association or care.

For a relationship or union with a flourish, the two accomplices must grasp the estimation of empathy and practice it energetically. The two accomplices ought to be inspired to learn and defeat any absence of sympathy.

Signs that you aren't getting empathy from your partner

On the off chance that you are an empathic and merciful individual, you may wind up working twofold time to be there for your loved one at whatever point the person needs you.

- You drop everything when your mate needs you. You tune in with empathy and love. You save your decisions and suppositions and enable your accomplice to completely express their sentiments.

- Your accomplice's agony causes you incredible torment. You endure when the individual in question endures.

- No matter what you do, your accomplice seldom responds. Actually, the person in question may see your feelings as minor, exaggerated, or disturbing.

- Your accomplice doesn't get on your outward appearances or temperaments since they are excessively caught up in personal worries. Your significant other doesn't set aside the effort to ask you examining inquiries or endeavor to comprehend the agony behind your terrible mind-set.

- Maybe your companion or accomplice sees your issues or stresses as less significant or difficult than their own. Instead of looking to all the more likely get you, your accomplice utilizes the chance to vent and think about their very own issues.

Some of the time a generally adoring and good-natured partner has an absence of empathy out of obliviousness or lack of mindfulness. Your accomplice may not be normally compassionate, and may not comprehend what empathy is and what it means for your relationship.

Maybe your accomplice never saw an empathic connection between their folks and never took in the aptitudes of sympathy.

Notwithstanding, it's conceivable that you are involved with somebody who has an absence of empathy. A narcissist needs empathy since they are too self-ingested, controlling, manipulative, and uncertain to offer you what you need in the relationship.

Dealing with narcissism in marriage

Recognize that narcissists aren't persuaded to change their conduct. For what reason would it be a good idea for them to be the length of they are getting their needs met?

This individual couldn't care less about improving the relationship or better understanding you by venturing into your perspective. He needs you to occupy his shoes consistently. She needs you to address every last bit of her issues and be accessible for her without using any passionate vitality consequently.

A genuine narcissist utilizes you to support their confidence and will once in a while see you as an equivalent. It's not healthy for your relationship in any way.

In the event that this is your circumstance, attempting to get your accomplice to indicate more compassion is a pointless activity.

You're the most logical option is to acknowledge that you won't get your passionate needs met by your accomplice or experience the delicacy and sympathy you want. You'll have to discover compassionate surrogates who can fill the excruciating hole and figure out how to deal with your very own passionate longings.

How to manage the lack of empathy from your partner?

When you need emotional assistance with empathy, don't keep attempting to cause them to get you or offer you the empathy you require. Your accomplices proceeded with childishness will just exacerbate you feel and undermine your confidence.

1. Quit making every effort to be available and accessible for your accomplice with the expectation that the person in question will respond. Your accomplice will keep on being an enthusiastic vampire, depleting you of the vitality you require to watch out for your own passionate needs.

2. Create or fortify your fellowships and associations with other grown-up relatives. Locate a couple of individuals with whom you have a sense of security to share your inward emotions — the individuals who have demonstrated compassion previously. Make certain to respond when they need you and your comprehension and backing.

3. Locate a minding, strong counselor who can be there for you during extremely troublesome or agonizing occasions. Your loved ones can't give the majority of your enthusiastic help, and since your life partner or accomplice is relationally repressed, you will require somebody who can fill in when you feel overpowered.

4. Practice self-empathy by focusing on your own misery and agony and offering yourself love and consideration.

Rationally step outside of yourself, as if you were your own closest companion or cherishing life partner, and give yourself the compassion you would offer others.

5. Tragically, as long as you are in a marriage with somebody who can't or reluctant to demonstrate your sympathy, the thoughts above won't enable you to make an all the more adoring, close, and empathic association with your accomplice.

6. You will either need to acknowledge an uneven association with a narrow-minded accomplice and adapt as well as can be expected, or settle on the troublesome choice to proceed onward and look for an association with somebody who doesn't need empathy.

In the event that your accomplice shows an ability to be progressively sympathetic and minding, at that point you have more to work with and a genuine chance to reinforce your marriage.

If you are one of the partners who are deprived of empathy, attempt these means in managing their absence of compassion:

1. Request that your accomplice read this post about compassion so the individual in question can more readily comprehend what it is and why it's such significant expertise for your marriage.

2. Tell your accomplice precisely how you need the person in question to be progressively sympathetic. Here and there you should be immediate instead of trusting your accomplice will intuit what you need.

3. Give your accomplice more understanding into your inward world and why you feel and react in the manner in which you do. Your accomplice may not understand why something causes you so much stress or torment or what may trigger these emotions except if you verbalize the more profound reasons.

4. Converse with your accomplice about your very own non-verbal communication and what it implies. Consider how you respond physically when you are baffled, harmed, or pitiful. What are your demeanors? How would you hold your body? Help your accomplice figure out how to peruse the physical indications of your feelings so the person can react with empathy.

5. Request that your accomplice maintains a strategic distance from decisions, spontaneous counsel, or genuine beliefs when you are communicating your sentiments or stresses. A sympathetic accomplice ought to tune in with open sympathy and delicacy and approve your emotions, regardless of whether the person in question doesn't concur with them.

6. Show more empathy toward your accomplice or companion. Perhaps the most ideal approaches to

encourage compassion is to be a decent model of it. Demonstrate your accomplice the sort of compassionate practices you need that person to demonstrate to you.

7. Recognize and recognition of your life partner when the individual shows compassion. Tell your accomplice how much their endeavors intend to you and how they bring you two closer. Everybody reacts well to encouraging feedback.

It might require some investment and persistence before they will defeat their absence of empathy and improve the relationship.

Here are some different ways you can turn out to be progressively empathic with your accomplice. If you want to show empathy to your partner, practice the following points.

1. Put yourself in your partner's shoes
Demonstrating empathy in a relationship can cement your accomplice's bond. That is the reason perhaps the most ideal approaches to be progressively compassionate is by basically envisioning yourself in their position and understanding what they feel like. A great beginning stage is to remind your partner to think about how they feel as they bear life's diverse emotions-- good, terrible and unbiased encounters. This activity will put down neural pathways that take into consideration an individual to understand – first their own, at that point that of another person.

2. Acknowledge their emotions

Upbeat couples frequently demonstrate their empathy by conveying verbally that they are setting aside the effort to envision what their accomplices are encountering. Notwithstanding tuning in, communicating to your partner that you comprehend what they're experiencing can demonstrate to them that you're in effect increasingly compassionate to their feelings rather than simply rejecting them.

3. Ask active questions

Being more adjusted with your accomplice's feelings can enable you to see when they're down before they even notice anything. When you begin to pose inquiries about their passionate state, it can demonstrate that you're put resources into their joy and in the relationship. They can pre-emptively ask their accomplices inquiries about how things are going, without holding back to be told.

4. Don't judge

A genuine association involves developing and adapting together. That implies helping each other out when they need it most, without making a decision about the other individual and making them feel little. They can retain judgment of their accomplice's decisions and accept that those decisions were made after cautious thought, paying little mind to whether they at last prompted achievement. Accepting that their accomplices are kind and clever people makes way for every single beneficial thing.

5. Share responsibilities

For long haul a connection, an incredible method to be increasingly sympathetic in a relationship is by just engrossing a portion of your accomplice's errands and everyday obligations. It can enable you to comprehend what they experience on every day and can enable you to quit judging. A fun method to demonstrate empathy in a long-haul relationship is to take on a portion of your accomplice's obligations regarding a timeframe.

6. Consider your better half's needs

Having empathy, or the capacity to look past your very own point of view, to that of an accomplice, advances basic leadership since it takes into account important thought of an accomplice's needs and needs before acting. Regardless of whether you purchase vegetables before they ask or you offer them an outing when they're feeling down, being on the ball with regards to your accomplice can enable them to feel nearer to you, which consequently, can make you more joyful.

7. Never stop being empathic

Regardless of whether you're in school or not, it's constantly a smart thought to adapt new things, particularly if it will profit your relationship. A few couples struggle while showing empathy toward each other on the grounds that having empathy is high-request relationship expertise that not every person has been educated or has set aside the effort to learn and ace. A lot of it can be attributed to the couples' individual exposure to empathic acts within their family when they were children.

8. Make sure to be with your loved one in hard times

Increasing comprehension of the critical estimation of exhibiting empathy towards an accomplice can urge couples to organize this relationship ability. Despite the fact that one accomplice is experiencing a hard time, which may slant their objectivity, they should attempt to turn out to be totally sensitive to their accomplices' sentiments in light of the conditions. This will end up being a nonstop two-way road, especially in light of the fact that one accomplice's difficult occasions regularly significantly affect different. While it's never simple to see your partner struggle with problems, which can in some cases cause conflict in a relationship, it's critical to be there for them notwithstanding during the hardest occasions. Envision yourself in their situation as opposed to guiding them to get over it.

9. Attempt to make progress

The thing about being empathic all the time is that it can turn out to be rationally debilitating. Your accomplice's feelings may turn into your feelings, as well. In a similar domain, attempt to indicate more empathy in your relationship to help lighten that. When you show empathy, you feel warm emotions and worry for your accomplice without overpowering yourself with taking their feelings. This is an incredible method to even now demonstrate sympathy without losing your own individual feeling of how you feel in some random circumstance.

While there are a lot of approaches to be there for your accomplice, having empathy for your better half's feelings and considerations can truly drive an association between both of you.

EMPATHY IN LOVE AND SEX

People reach out far and wide for the way to a sound, fulfilling sexual coexistence. Some people take part routinely in—and even commit their lives to—the everlasting discourse encompassing sexual fulfillment and delight.

We humans as a whole are mind-boggling, entrancing sexual creatures and the best way to comprehend and appreciate each other explicitly is to have empathy and the capacity to comprehend and share the sentiments of another—close to the individuals we share our bodies with. It bodes well, considering sex should be commonly pleasurable and fulfilling; in any case, it appears to be dreadfully uncommon that we put ourselves in the enthusiastic, physical and mental prosperity of the individuals with whom we take part in such an exceptionally personal act.

Who is a sexual empath?

Compassion is one of the most significant capacities that help individuals see one another. So for what reason is it significantly increasingly significant in your relationship? And who is a sexual empath?

An empath is portrayed as somebody who can get on and is delicate to the enthusiastic or mental condition of someone else. A sexual empath can be described as somebody whose empathic capacities heighten during a sensual experience so the individual in question detects more pressure or delight. A sexual empath is more tuned in to these emotions than even an ordinary empath. Sexual empaths are profoundly sensitive during lovemaking. In short, a sexual empath is somebody whose empathic capacities strengthen during a sexual experience. They are exceptionally delicate during sex and even snapshots of a tease, regularly encountering elevated pressure or ecstasy. They are more mindful of their accomplice's feelings than expected, and to feel their best, they should figure out how to impart physical closeness to somebody who can respond to their adoration and regard.

The truth is that there is no single method to have a decent sexual coexistence. A few people need sex toys, others prefer BDSM, a few people need to begin laying down with an alternate sexual orientation, a few people need to move out and explore intimacy with different people and others simply need to begin jerking off.

While sex itself is a pleasurable experience, why sexual empathy is important? Why some people have great sexual experiences over time, while others don't?

It appears that in numerous occasions, individuals go into sexual relationships bearing in mind the end goal of the sex being great immediately. Sadly, sex can't turn out to be great without correspondence and understanding, the two of which require some degree of enthusiastic closeness with our sexual accomplices. Regardless of whether correspondence happens the absolute first time, the straightforward certainty that exchange happened implies you have turned out to be closer with that individual than you have with a great many people throughout your life.

We're all human. To expect that a specific degree of enthusiastic powerlessness doesn't go before great sex is a supposition that will set you up for disillusionment and disappointment.

To get proper feedback from our sexual partners, we should learn to be empathic. We need to think about our weaknesses and insecurities about sex and pleasure our partners. We need to ask each other what we need, what feels better and what doesn't, because, without compassion, communication is almost difficult to accomplish.

However, we can't simply ask. We need to think about the feedback we get. We need to mind that sex feels great for our accomplices, as opposed to painful and dissatisfying. We need to think about our accomplices having orgasms. Not only that, we need to comprehend if our partners aren't in the mindset, then we need to analyze our situation and theirs as well. We need to quit being insensible to the point that we'd want to have intercourse with individuals.

Notwithstanding during a passing sexual experience with an outsider, having empathy toward your partner grants you the chance to turn out to be increasingly experienced and see progressively about how an individual's body functions. You get the chance to leave liking what you took part because you gave joy, delight and opened your psyche up to finding out about the inclinations of an individual other than yourself.

Empathy is the motivation behind why we long to engage in sexual relations with genuine, live individuals. Compassion is the motivation behind why pornography, vibrating dildos, telephone sex, strip clubs, and different substitutes simply don't work for the vast majority. The more sympathy that is associated with sexual experience, the better the sex will be for the two gatherings. Having compassion toward your accomplice implies you get to encounter your pleasure, however the joy of another genuine individual.

Effect of Sexual Empathy and Empaths

While heightened sentiments of pleasure seem like a distant dream, this isn't generally the situation. Sexual empaths can frequently get excessively cleared up by the rush of another sexual relationship since it feels so exceptional. On the off chance that somebody tags along who starts their sexuality, they are so anxious to enter a relationship, they overlook natural cautioning signs. So they take part in a sexual relationship at an early stage with an individual who's a poor decision.'

Rather than agreeing to simply anybody, one can step away for a while from searching for the right sexual partner and rather dedicating your energy during the act. This is how, when somebody who is truly well-coordinated to you goes along, you can believe that you're not blinded by sensation and rather settling on a positive choice. Empaths lead to blooming of much-needed sexual pleasure. Whenever sex, soul, and heart are consolidated in lovemaking, it is a brilliant experience together.

Keeping up a Solid Relationship Through Setting Limits

When you're seeing someone, recommends being observant of your accomplice's mental and emotional state. If your partner has had a troublesome day and is irate, it probably won't be the best time to be sexual since empaths can ingest this annoyance. You have to talk honestly to your partner about this. Your cherished needs to comprehend for what reason you're deciding not to be personal when the individual in question is furious or under outrageous pressure.

Regardless of whether you're single, dating, or in a long haul relationship, sex is a significant point to talk about—particularly in case you're an empath or profoundly sensitive individual.

Since empaths are delicate to vitality, there is nothing of the sort as "easy-going sex." During lovemaking, energies join; we can get both uneasiness and happiness from our sexual accomplice, and regularly sense their considerations and sentiments. That is the reason we should pick our accomplices astutely—something else, sex can be loaded up with lethal vitality, stress, or dread—especially on the off chance that we are a sexual empath.

Sexual empaths dread that since it has taken such a long time to discover somebody even remotely intriguing, they have to stay with this individual regardless of the warnings. In any case, we open ourselves to superfluous hurt when we become appended to inaccessible individuals who simply don't want to cherish us back.

Rather than simply trusting that the correct individual will appear, find out about the intensity of our sexual vitality.

When we've discovered the correct accomplice, the reason for closeness is to join our heart vitality with our sexual vitality. Empaths blossom with heart vitality; when sex, soul, and heart are consolidated during lovemaking, it is wonderfully nurturing.

EMPATHY IN PARENTING

Empathy has never been progressively essential, yet the capacity to see how others feel can be supported. It's up to the grown-ups not to allow let our future generation be insensitive, or worse, turn into narcissists. There is no absence of the bounty of advice when it comes to child-rearing. Be that as it may, it appears to be evident that if needed the world to be a superior place, we do need to sustain sensitivity and empathy in our children. As talked about before, kids who experience empathic surroundings are the ones who will have sympathy towards others when they grow up.

Some pieces of advice center around expanding enthusiastic education as a rule, by helping children to all the more likely comprehend their feelings and the feelings of others. Others include helping children to cultivate a feeling of themselves as minding individuals, by connecting with them in exercises where they can be liberal and by demonstrating liberality toward others ourselves. Still, others include helping children to end up good legends, in school and out of it.

For instance, you can help children build up an ethical character. It is your duty as an empath. Children who are lauded for helping other people are more averse to act more liberally later on than children who were commended for being having empathy towards others. We have to help children build up an ethical personality, not simply commend them for good deeds. To react empathically, kids must consider themselves to be individuals who care and worth others' worries and feelings. Missing that vital piece leaves an immense void in a child's empathic character.

Also, giving them second chances is yet another benefit which you will be providing to your children. It's not in every case simple to get children to take another's point of view. When they talk or act uncaringly, it very well may be useful to enable children to have second chances as opposed to just rebuffing them. You can highlight uncaring behavior and assess how unfeeling influences others, thus helping your children to comprehend another's point of view. Then comes the action part where the child must be taught to repair the hurt and present appropriate reparations. One can teach them to express frustration for cutthroat conduct while focusing on desires for minding conduct later on. Try to search for those control minutes when we can enable our youngsters to get a handle on how their activities influence others so it extends their compassion, and one day they can act directly without our direction. Learning empathy is essential for children's character to develop and help them live a satisfying life ahead without being exploited.

Empathy Lessons Begins at Home First

Parents are children's first school. Adults must help children learn empathy through play-acting, and books and other activities that let them get inside the characters' brains.

Exercises that permit cautious reflection on how others are feeling in a given circumstance help manufacture the abilities required for good activity. For instance, reading books is found to be effective in inculcating empathy in children. The correct book can blend a kid's sympathy superior to anything any exercise or talk ever could. What's more, the correct book coordinated with the correct kid can be the passage to opening their heart to humankind. Of course, you can throw in some wisdom of yours to avoid toxic empathy which will ruin them.

All things considered, over and over again these are disengaged endeavors by individual instructors or schools. Some portion of the issue comes from our excessively aggressive culture, and the way that numerous children are pushed to succeed scholastically as opposed to pushed to be kinder, better individuals. Regardless of whether parents state they value thoughtfulness and empathy, if they just acclaim accomplishment, they give an inappropriate impression to their children. If we are serious about raising a sympathetic, empathic child, at that point our desires must be a great deal more clear to our children. Also, seeing how graciousness benefits youngsters and gives them a preferred position for progress and bliss may be simply the help to alter our own particular way of living.

To build up the ability to feel empathy for other people, a youngster must feel seen, felt, heard, and comprehended by in any event one essential parental figure. Relatives who know, acknowledge, and regard a youngster paying little mind to outside achievements help that child feel genuinely appreciated by their adult family members. These sorts of connections increase a child's capacity to think about others.

There are some important steps which must be taken to ensure that your child grows up to be a compassionate individual

-Ingrain empathy at home

Families impart empathy at home by providing chances to rehearse sympathy, helping kids experience kindness and teaching youngsters to self-control their feelings. Peruse progressively about sympathy.

-Sustain positive citizenship

Bringing up children to observe kindness does not happen by coincidence. It happens when they connect with others out of luck, confront moral difficulties, reflect on their qualities, notice how social issues are associated, and create positive and energetic inspirational figures.

-Undivided attention

Undivided attention is a training that enables guardians and youngsters to develop in their comprehension of one another. Three aptitudes regularly connected with great listening are--- respect the other individual, listening more than talking, and looking towards understanding others. Whenever you and your kid experience issues tuning in, attempt a straightforward listening activity created by the family advisor,

-Show kids why giving back pays

Families who show mindfulness, collaboration, empathy, benevolence, cooperation, and the significance of coexisting with others are ground-breaking compassion manufacturers. As children are growing up, they ought to advance through three formative stages as they take on jobs in the public arena: being mindful residents; improving their networks; and contributing to taking care of cultural issues. Being social pays as the child learns a lot. If they see empathy in others, chances are that they will adopt the same state of mind.

-Show a progressive outlook

Tell your kid that compassion is anything but a fixed characteristic—that it creates after some time. Empathy can be expanded with training simply. The more you practice, the better you will be at understanding another's considerations and emotions.

-Open them to various perspectives

At the point when families develop an interest in how people and gatherings of individuals see the world in an unexpected way, they grow youngsters' erudite person, relational, and passionate limits. They help kids perceive and comprehend contrasting points of view. At the point when tested to investigate partialities, discover shared characteristics, and gather importance from what they envision life might be want to stroll in someone else's shoes, youngsters fabricate a more noteworthy limit with regards to sympathy.

-Reconsider how children learn benevolence

It is nothing unexpected that grown-ups like themselves when they show consideration to their kids and grandkids. Not exclusively do great deeds make us feel much improved, \yet individuals who are thoughtful and empathic are frequently the best. All things considered, we don't satisfy youngsters when we just empower them to be collectors of thoughtfulness. We increase their sentiments of joy, improve their prosperity, decrease painful emotions, enhance their friendships, and construct harmony by instructing them to be providers of benevolence.

-Communication during family gatherings

Blessing giving during special events such as festivals and birthdays can shape your child's long-lasting personalities. The qualities your family holds about blessing giving can be transformed into ground-breaking exercises that show sympathy, compassion, and consideration. Be proactive about your qualities as you create occasions which are saturated with positive feelings. Incorporate kids in discussions about how to provide for other people. Peruse increasingly about blessing giving.

-Help children gain from volunteering

Children increase formative advantages by taking an interest in building and nurturing connections. Tweens and teenagers are particularly prepared to embrace kindness when they are taken out by parent figures and watch them helping others. In any case, to do as such, they need grown-up help and support. It is important to realize why taking out your child for volunteering can enable them to take full advantage of their experiences.

-Lead with compassion

Parents need to step up as the inspirational figures for their children. At the point when guardians lead with empathy, appreciation, and benevolence, children figure out how to do likewise. It is essential to figure out how to be well-spoken and express your family esteems with the goal that kids comprehend and gain from them.

-Talk about cash and generosity

Each discussion about money is additionally about qualities. Giving is about liberality. Work is about determination." The more children learn about money management since the beginning, the more they can add to family discussions that tap into the benefits of giving. These discourses can enable youngsters to place themselves in others' shoes and help them experience the joy of giving without damaging their finances.

The seed of empathy has to be planted at the earlier stage, and then it will bear the fruits of empathy. Your child and you can be agents of change in this increasingly insensitive world.

Empathy in Friendships

In the beginning periods of friendships, it very well may be anything but difficult to put together your association concerning straightforward unity and fun. For a more profound, progressively significant enthusiastic bond, in any case, you need a firm handle on empathy. Empathy in a kinship will assist you with getting each other through troublesome occasions just as hold each other under tight restraints. Simultaneously, figuring out how to develop your compassionate comprehension of a companion can enable you to extend your comprehension of one another.

There is a way you can be empathic to your friend. Figure out how to abstain from offering guidance or attempting to fix their issues when they come to you simply needing understanding. Offer empathy as your regular behavior and shun offering guidance and arrangements except if your friend asks you legitimately. For instance, in some situations, your friend may ask for advice or pose questions like, "What can I do now?" Otherwise, expect that they are searching for a shoulder to lean on and you are their choice. Keep in mind that empathy helps individuals through disturbing and troublesome circumstances by helping them feel they don't need to confront their torment alone. Help them realize that their sentiments are typical and reasonable to other people. This will engage them to deal with their feelings maturely and settle on their own choices about what to do.

How to Use Empathy to Help your Friend?

-Echo their emotions

Figure out how to express your empathy by resounding your companion's sentiments back to him in your very own words. This activity not just offers a voice to the compassion you feel, it will assist you with growing more grounded sympathy for them. Reword their emotions, yet besides, help them to end up mindful of sentiments they might battle with. In unstable circumstances, help them to evade rash activities by keeping them concentrated on comprehension and handling their emotions instead of concentrating outward on individuals who they feel have wronged them.

-Creative mind

Utilize your creative mind to enable you to empathize completely and effectively. Put yourself in your friend's shoes and envision how they would feel and think in the circumstances they are facing. Full empathy requires envisioning the occasions existing apart from everything else, except attempting to envision how it would feel to be them as far as how their background has affected them. This requires seeing how your background has impacted you and how your emotional pattern is not the same as theirs. You will always be unable to completely comprehend someone else's understanding, yet the more subtleties and contrasts you can consider, the more grounded your sympathy will be.

-Confinements

Regard the confinements of your sympathy. Realize that you may not generally comprehend what a companion feels and may need to tune in with a receptive outlook in circumstances where their sentiments are confounding to you. Pose inquiries, particularly on occasion when your efforts to understand them might end up disappointing them rather than making a difference. Perceive that they likewise must help cross over any barrier when you two don't see one another.

-Body language

Utilize nonverbal communication that communicates to your companion that you are focusing on them. Keep up eye to eye connection, don't fold your arms or tap your foot and lean internal when your companion is talking. These sign will demonstrate your companion that you are centered on them and care about what is being said. Seeming occupied - regardless of whether you are not - may appear to be egotistical or cold-hearted.

-Rewording sentences

Reword what your friend has quite recently let you know however make a point to utilize diverse wording. This demonstrates you were tuning in and comprehend the message that your friend is attempting to confer. It will likewise help clear things up if you didn't completely get a handle on what your friend was attempting to state, and avert future miscommunication.

-Verbalize

Verbalize how you accept your friend is feeling. An expression pursued by an exact feeling demonstrates your partner that you get it. This central idea of empathy is significant because imparting emotions to a friend fortifies the obligation of kinship.

Your companion may quit communicating emotions to you if they figure you don't appreciate what is being talked about.

-Clarify if not understanding

Clarify that you comprehend why your friend would feel that way. Relate your friend's present inclination to a circumstance in your very own life that caused a comparative feeling in you and discussion about how you took care of it. Demonstrating your companion that you have experienced comparative circumstances and felt a similar way will further underline what you share practically speaking and help reinforce the obligation of your kinship.

Compassion is an enthusiastic response to the situation of others. Sympathy can prompt unselfish conduct, for example helping somebody with the sole goal of improving that individual's prosperity. On the off chance that we see individuals in trouble, for instance, we feel similar feelings, and this may provoke us to support them. However, the connection between compassion and charitableness is still a long way from clear. When we help companions out of luck, we are provoked by sentiments of empathy, and that when we help relatives we do as such because we have desires for correspondence.

Why do some people help friends more than families?

We as a whole contrast ourselves and the individuals around us, yet few people do this more than others. At the point when the individuals in this gathering contrast themselves and somebody in a more awful position, they regularly experience negative feelings, for example, strain, disturbance, nervousness, and aggravation.' These negative feelings are a statement of empathy. These individuals feel engaged with the individual out of luck and relate to them. The negative feelings are a method for communicating this. But haven't we observed that some people help friends more than families, especially when we are not obliged to help them.

There is an explanation for this. Friends are family we choose not out of an obligation arising out of blood relation. We help companions for unexpected reasons in comparison to relatives. Individuals help companions out of sentiments of empathy, yet they help relatives since they have assumptions regarding responses. It was constantly expected that empathy was principally normal for family connections. Be that as it may, it makes sense when you consider it. You can, as a rule, depend on family. We don't pick our families, yet we do pick our friends. We feel a more prominent feeling of association with companions, so sentiments of empathy are progressively significant.

Empathy patterns differ from people to people. That makes it increasingly hard to examine charitableness. There is a model for this called 'unselfish decision model'. The model fills in as pursues. You see the pain of others and this prompts a sentiment of empathy, over which you have no control. This can be trailed by different emotional reactions: identifying/relating to the individual being referred to, concern or 'considerate nature' (delicate sentiments). These are reactions that we can impact. These reactions can prompt empathy and selflessness, for example understanding the other individual's anguish and the ability to mitigate it. Charitableness is a choice and something that we can effectively develop when we watch others in the problem.

Sadly, unselfishness is underestimated in our general public. We are pack creatures. We can't exist without social contact, so it is no outrage if we are eager to help one another. You are not obliged to help others, but still, you do. Selflessness makes the world an increasingly lovely place. It is remunerating to support somebody. 'A few people say, in this manner, that helping other people depends on narrow-minded thought processes. On the off chance that you help somebody and it has positive ramifications for you, that does not intend to state that your basic thought processes are not charitable.

Chapter 5: The Plight of Empaths

While empathy can offer importance to our lives, it is warned that it can likewise turn out badly if a line isn't drawn. While demonstrating an empathetic reaction to the disaster and misfortune of others can be useful, it can likewise, whenever misled, transform us into emotional parasites.

When empaths lose track of reasonable empathetic response, it can lead to several negative impacts on their lives. It is good to be good, but too good never did well to anyone.

Sympathy can aggravate individuals, so on the off chance that they erroneously see that someone else is compromising an individual they care for. Hostility may arise as one may misinterpret the intentions of others. For instance, if someone is trying to hug your child, an empath (being too sensitive) may wrongly read another person as a threat. Although you are trying to protect your child, your paranoia might turn out into an inconvenience for the person whose intentions were not malicious. Thus, sympathy and hostility are also described as "existential twins."

Not only that, empaths tend to lose money more than usual; sometimes, to the point where they end up penniless. For a considerable length of time, instances of excessively compassionate people imperiling the prosperity of themselves and their families by giving ceaselessly their life investment funds to destitute people have served as the prime example. Such excessively compassionate individuals who feel they are by one way or another in charge of the misery of others have built up empathy-based blame.

The blame goes on to the point of self-ridicule as well. The state of "survivor blame" is a type of sympathy based blame in which an empathic individual erroneously feels that their very own satisfaction has come at the expense or may have even caused someone else's wretchedness. People who normally carry on of compassion-based blame, or neurotic philanthropy, will, in general, create gentle discouragement in later-life.

Since money is involved, it must be remembered that a lot of us have families who need our care, empathy, and love. The neurotic philanthropy can damage relationships if an intervention is not sought. The main thing which must be remembered is that empathy ought to never be mistaken for affection. Love isn't enough to cement the bonds; stable and better finances play a massive role as well. While love can make any relationship better, empathy can't. Love can fix, compassion can't. One who is getting involved in empathetic spending must carefully weigh their priorities. For instance of how even good-natured empathy can harm a relationship, we must look around ourselves.

Not only do people end up being bankrupt while trying to help others, but the vines of empathy can also wrap onto their physical, mental and emotional states. Empathy fatigue or weariness" alludes to a condition of physical fatigue coming about because of rehashed or delayed individual inclusion in the constant sickness, incapacity, injury, distress, and loss of others. An empath can become so involved in the welfare of others that they may forget their well-being. Any excessively sympathetic individual can encounter compassion exhaustion.

On top of it, if an empath encounters a narcissist, it's done for. So, we need to understand the opposite side as well.

Narcissism

As a matter of first importance, we have to comprehend what are narcissism, abuse, and narcissistic abuse to understand how they can damage empaths.

Narcissistic Personality Disorder alludes to self-important conduct, an absence of compassion for other individuals, and a requirement for the reverence which must all be reliably clear at work and seeing someone. Narcissistic individuals are much of the time depicted as arrogant, conceited, manipulative, and needy. Narcissists may focus on impossible individual results and might be persuaded that they merit exceptional treatment. Narcissism is a variant of Narcissistic Personality Disorder. It includes presumptuousness, manipulative nature, childishness, linear thought processes, and vanity-adoration for mirrors.

Narcissists will, in general, have high confidence. Be that as it may, narcissism isn't simply something very similar regard; individuals who have high confidence are frequently unassuming, though narcissists once in a while are. It was once imagined that narcissists have high confidence superficially, yet where it counts they are uncertain. Nonetheless, the narcissists are secure or self-important at the two levels. Spectators may construe that instability is there because narcissists will, in general, be cautious when their confidence is undermined or they are being criticized; narcissists can be hostile when they feel that they are being attacked. They tend to read between the lines a lot more than necessary. The occasionally hazardous way of life may all the more by and large reflect sensation-chasing or impulsivity such as reckless spending. Narcissists don't need empathy in the manner we commonly accept – they need empathy, regret, and lament-- all of which they lack.

In the previous chapter, we learned that a lot of us equate feelings like sympathy with empathy; however as referenced over, an individual can comprehend what someone else feels, thinks, and encounters without inclination the human feelings that accompany it. Narcissists lack it. So, it will, in general, let them free for harmful conduct. The narcissist's absence of compassion thought infers that their oppressive conduct is unexpected. It's amazingly manipulative and very purposeful when they are dealing with people who are highly receptive of them, especially the empaths.

Empaths Facing Narcissist Abuse

Individuals who are shafts separated may be drawn together for all inappropriate reasons. The pairing of an empath and a narcissist is a 'poisonous' fascination bound for disaster.

Most of the times, empaths embrace people's emotions and needs as they have been in a condition, in childhood or somewhere when they were growing up. There are a good number of chances that empaths are the way they are as they have been in a condition of vulnerability or tragedy, and as a result, they have experienced such a great amount of pain that they basically surrender their self-sufficiency, go beyond their financial and emotional means to help others, and do not take a stand for themselves even at the cost of emotional harm. Also called "learned helplessness," it can prompt gloom and other psychological maladjustments. And it is the most lucrative playground for narcissists. Narcissists, for instance, are pulled in to individuals they will get the best use from. Frequently, this implies they seek after and target empaths.

If a narcissist needs to constrain their subject into learned helplessness, the initial step is to set up an association. And empaths, being compassionate, almost always are willing to lend an ear for the distressed person, who could or could not be narcissistic. Intellectual sympathy is a narcissist's weapon for setting up the association.

As should be obvious, the narcissist's absence of empathy is a fantasy since they have to utilize psychological compassion to get what they need from everyone around them. They utilize Emotional Empathy to get what they want, and they do not care about the effect on other people. When someone is desperate for support or assistance or in serious circumstances, they utilize psychological sympathy to get into the subject's head. They have to comprehend the subject's sentiments and thoughts which they would then be able to control into creating a result that is most useful to them. Convenient, isn't it?

That is the reason you've likely wound up bobbing forward and backward commonly pondering about what they feel for you. Narcissists keep empaths on edge. It is much simpler to accept this isn't deliberate. However, these activities are determined. Narcissists decipher feelings like love, receptiveness, thoughtfulness, and liberality as shortcomings. Also, on the off chance that you offer a bit of leeway, they'll take a mile, back up, and travel a similar mile again and again until you're hauling your hair out.

What narcissists see in empaths is a giving, cherishing individual who is going to be dedicated, adoring and most genuine shoulder to lean upon. The very fact that an empathetic person is willing to hear them out makes them alert and interested. Be that as it may, sadly empaths are pulled in to narcissists because from the outset this is about a bogus self. Narcissists present a bogus self, where they can appear to be enchanting and shrewd, and notwithstanding giving until you don't do things their way, and after that they get cold, retaining and rebuffing."

Empaths are something contrary to narcissists. While individuals with narcissistic character issue have no compassion and flourish with the requirement for profound respect, empaths are exceptionally touchy and tuned in to other individuals' feelings. In a way, empaths are like sponges that absorb sentiments from other individuals in all respects effectively. This makes them appealing to narcissists since they see somebody who will satisfy their every need in a benevolent manner.

At the point when a narcissist is attempting to snare somebody in, they will love and mindful, yet their veil soon begins to slip. Toward the starting, they just observe the great characteristics and accept the friendship that will make them look great. This doesn't last since narcissists tend to be loaded with hatred, and they consider most to be as beneath them. When they begin to see their accomplice's faults, they never again deal nicely with them, and soon begin to reprimand them for not being impeccable.

It can at times take some time for the real nature to appear. In any case, this conflicts with an empath's responses, as they believe they can fix individuals and mend anything with empathy. They truly have faith that they can listen more and give more. That is not the situation with a narcissist. And the empaths have a hard time facing that other person is devoid of compassion. It's unbelievable for some empaths that someone simply doesn't have compassion, and that they can't mend the other individual with their affection.

Empaths buckle down for concordance, though narcissists are hoping to do the inverse. They appreciate disorder and like to realize they can pull an individual's strings. This is a strategy narcissists use to reel their accomplice back in. With empaths, it is exceptionally powerful; because they need to help their accomplice and help them develop. Eventually, they are simply being abused further.

Narcissists' strategies on empaths

Narcissists control empaths by leading them on with irregular expectations. They will incorporate compliments and thoughtfulness into their conduct, causing the empathetic individual to accept that if they carry on in the right way, they will recover the happiness of others. And that is what empaths believe in doing. Sad, but a dangerous combination.

The push and pull nature of the narcissistic relationship can create a damaging partnership between the person in question and the abuser, where it can feel practically difficult to leave the relationship, regardless of how much harm it is doing.

With compassion comes the capacity and readiness to take a gander at ourselves and take a gander at our deficiencies and that gets exploited while the toxic bond is going on. It turns into a cycle for an empath who has been immune to self-damage because they begin taking a gander at themselves, and what do they have to do to change, and what do they have to do must be beneficial to others. It's the ideal set up, lamentably.

Evading the cycle of abuse

Besides, the cycle continues until the Empath lose the sense of who they are any more, and feels incredibly exhausted, self-ridiculing and disheartened from endeavoring and missing the mark with the Narcissist over and over. They feel exhausted and disheartened while continuing to evade and redirect their feelings towards themselves to keep up the bond and benefit others. The precise inverse thing they have to do is hurt their tricky Narcissist, who will quickly use the empath's outward renunciation of anger to demonstrate how hurt they have been by them, and as evidence for them being the veritable Narcissist.

The key to an Empath truly vanquishing this cycle and being adequately ready to leave, and retouch, is to truly re-perceive themselves with and feel their annoyance, and recognize that they in conviction cause hurt, and are in like manner allowed to feel rage, and lose their patience and care. That, without a doubt, it is okay to use unskilful or inadequate strategies in characterizing a resentment awakened point of confinement. It is acceptable to anger the narcissist if the latter is to make certain authoritatively going to have their feelings hurt anyway. That every so often it is critical to use ill will and capacity to get someone to finally back off, in case they have felt equipped for your essentialness, time, and resources, and this doesn't make someone Narcissistic, problematic, or entitled, yet rather is verification of confidence and regard.

Chapter 6: Personal emotional healing solutions

Empaths find it hard to protect themselves. Hence, they must understand when to stop others from exploiting their genuine emotions. Since they usually absorb others' energies, it can be hard for them to distinguish between their feelings and those of others.

An indication that you are holding someone's feelings is when you experience a sudden distinction mental or physical state when you are around a particular individual Almost certainly, if you didn't feel tense, disheartened, drained, or cleared out already, the trouble is at any rate generally beginning from the individual being referred to.

In case you move away and the trouble hits you, it is not yours. The identification of problems is one aspect; one true question is how an empath gets rid of them?

How empaths heal themselves?

1. **Go into Your Pain Rather Than Trying to Escape from It**

   It sounds irrational, doesn't it--going into your emptiness. Nevertheless, it's a huge development for releasing the built-up emotions inside you. When we are diverted with sidestepping, checking and avoiding our desolation, we continue the cycle of our pain. Instead of respecting the impulse to run – stop – stay there. Plunk down and let yourself feel the shortcoming, the confusion, the disappointment, the hurt. Just once you face the truth of the pain you feel you can then head to the period of discharging the suffering.

2. **Breathe in and reiterate your realization to counter negative emotions**

As you breathe in, the force of your voice can channel the uneasiness out of your body. Your breath is the vehicle that transports it back to the universe.

Say, "I release you." Also, while saying this, you can expressly breathe in deadly emotions out of your lumbar spine in your lower back. The spaces between your vertebrae are useful to be utilized as channels for getting rid of disastrous feelings. Imagine the burden of leaving through these spaces in your spine.

3. **Securing Is Not a Useful Technique**

As a fleeting method, ensuring can be helpful; anyway, it's not a whole deal course of action. Securing to "secure" yourself beforehand and how it uses the language of victimhood which is counterproductive to transforming into a repaired empath. Securing is essentially about restricting either people's imperativeness and resistance just serves to continue with the cycles of fear and pain inside. Instead of fighting with what you are feeling, open yourself. Empower yourself to experience the emotions, yet furthermore, let them pass by not holding onto them as yours. This requires huge speculation and practice. In any case, non-association is an incredibly improved whole deal course of action.

4. **Step away from the source of disturbance**

Move away several feet from the suspected source of negative energy. Check whether you feel light. Make an effort not to worry over at fault outcasts. Wherever you are, don't hesitate to change your place. Move to an undeniably quiet place as soon as possible. Don't worry about what others will think of you. It's fine to stand up for yourself and give yourself the approval to move. It's called self-care and there is no harm in that. Empaths much of the time end up in overwhelming social conditions. If that unfolds, make a point to take out time to recharge yourself. Once you feel fine, you can return to the gathering.

5. **Purgation and Body-Mindfulness**

As an empath, it is basic to the point that you intertwine some reliable decontamination into your common regular practice to free yourself of the suffocating emotions you may harbor. Favored sorts of cleansing methods among empaths are journaling, walking and running. Various kinds of purgation consist of singing, walking, yelling (furtively), laughing and crying. It is in like manner unfathomably significant as an empath to tell yourself the best way to connect with your body. This is called body-care or physical consideration. Making sense of how to be in contact with your body is an incredible technique for protecting and building up yourself right rather than getting to be stirred up in the flood of emotions and vibes that come to your course. Body-care is also a not too bad technique for making sense of how to check out your needs, similarly as continuing and managing yourself.

6. **Avoid most extreme physical contact**

Emotions travel through the eyes and contact. If you're absorbing negative energy from someone, limit eye to eye contact, including grasps and hand-holding. In spite of the way that grasping a companion or relative in a tough situation routinely helps you feel good. However, do not go near if you are affected by it. You can continue sending positive vibrations from a distance.

7. **Detoxification in water**

Detoxification in water is one of the most effective ways empaths can recharge themselves. Water is a life-giving element. Using some essential oil drops and healing salts can help you calm especially when you have faced a tiring and exhausting day.

If this is not working for you, there is always another way. You can go for water-based spa treatments. The perfect empath release works best in normal mineral springs that flush out all of that causes trouble to you.

8. **Set limits and cut-off points**

There's no way to get around it. To suffer and thrive, you have quite far with people. Don't be someone's venting bucket. Always make sure that you spend less time taking staying concerned about another person. It's perfectly fine to say no. Simply telling them that you don't want to talk or communicate at the moment is perfectly fine. Remember, your purpose is to protect yourself, not fall into the trap of so-called emotional vampires. It's possible that they don't realize it, but you can. Changing the pattern of communicating with your friends or acquaintances would certainly be helpful to you. You can be empathic without staying too much in contact. That way you would not only help yourself but them too.

9. **Set aside a few minutes to regroup**

   The main strength of empaths comes from their ability to connect with others even though they are the ones to bear the brunt in the end. Spending alone time without any interference helps an empath reconnect with their ability and recharge themselves. It's important to be alone without anyone around to interrupt your flow of unidirectional thoughts. Keep everyone aside and think of yourself. You are your best friend and caretaker first. You won't face any harm in spending some alone time. Respond only when some critical issue comes up and needs your instant attention. Once again, you are the one to define what is critical to you.

10. **Take a break from social media**

    You need a standard break from social media that saturates you with an unreasonable measure of information. Online media triggers your emotions, for instance, Twitter social affairs, Instagram, unpleasant news channels—can cripple your ability to fall asleep. It's not hard to get emotional in the virtual world, so put aside a couple of minutes for yourself.

11. **Spend time and energy in nature and work on 'earthing' yourself**

From soil we came; to the soil, we will go back. There is hardly an empath who doesn't love connecting with the earthly elements. Empaths love nature and feel calm there. The Earth transmits healing. Go to grassland and lay down with your hands and legs stretched. Try to absorb the natural emotions in your entire body and connect them with the vibrations of soil. Go shoeless. Walk barefoot. Channel others' negative energies, feel the grass between your exposed toes, walk around the sand or the soil.

Realizing the gift of empathy

With training, enabled empaths can mend, venture, work with, and intensify emotional energy. Indeed, even without preparing, those skilled with empathy are profoundly sensitive to the feelings of others. At the point when individuals are feeling happy, cherishing, energized, or tranquil, empaths can feel it. Then again, when individuals are feeling pitiful, irate, alarmed, or lethargic, empaths feel that as well.

More than monitoring feelings, empaths absorb feelings intuitively, especially negative feelings. Individuals experiencing melancholy frequently feel better in the wake of being around empaths in light of how they naturally siphon away negative feelings. This is extraordinary for anybody with gloom, yet to some degree risky for an untrained empath.

Numerous empaths are helpless before their blessing and live subject to the enthusiastic climate made by everyone around them. The endowment of empathy consequently brings mindfulness and absorption of feeling yet no learning of how to manage it a short time later. Be that as it may, similar to some other blessing, compassion can be an amazing resource when it is appropriately prepared. With training, empaths can change the feeling they retain, recuperate the feelings in others, use feelings to power show, and even effectively venture more joyful passionate atmospheres.

At the point when individuals talk about being an empath, it is regularly with a feeling of pain. At the point when empathy is untrained, it very well may overpower to feel and assimilate to such an extent. It can be overwhelming for many untrained empaths who don't know how to properly utilize their gift. If you are one of them, do not be afraid. Your answers are out there. Keep in mind that you are the core of humankind, and you are a healer who will heal the world.

Chapter 7: Empath Strategies

There are three important strategies which empaths can use to help those in distress. These techniques help empaths normalizing and maintain their gift without putting themselves in problems.

- **Liquid Empathy**

Before working with empathy, utilize this procedure to help deal with your inexperience. At whatever point you feel mysteriously pitiful, apprehensive, or angry out of the blue, you can utilize the liquid sympathy procedure to free yourself of these feelings and help you become accustomed to working with enthusiastic vitality.

Empaths are intended to fill in as the core of mankind. They can feel the feelings of others since we are intended to heal and work with them. Looking at the situation objectively, this implies they can work with and control emotional energy. They can take in emotional energy, yet that does not imply that they need to get a hold of it.

So, take a full breath and look inside yourself. Know about any negative feelings keeping you down. Negative emotional energy will, in general, be substantial, cloying, and dim. The weight is the sign. To state that a feeling is substantial infers that it reacts to gravity. It does.

So now grab hold of all the substantial, negative energy within yourself, and send it where it needs to go. Send it to the focal point of the Earth. The Earth's center is hot and liquid. It can separate and dissolve any component into its most perfect structure. On the off chance that the core can soften overwhelming metals, it can positively liquefy down negative vitality.

So push, channel, and siphon any negative energy inside you down into the Earth. See it move through the ground past the roots and earth, past layers of fossil and coal, lastly arrive at fluid hot magma. The negative energy is disintegrated with extreme heat and light, and the antagonism blurs away to discover just harmony. You in the interim, feel lighter than you would have suspected conceivable.

Practice this strategy regularly. The more you do, the better control you will pick up the emotional condition you live in. When you deal with it, you can attempt effectively depleting negative feelings surrounding you before they even touch you.

- **Projective empathy**

This procedure is valuable when somebody is experiencing negative feelings and you need to enable them to feel good. If somebody feels disappointed, angry or furious, you could dissolve or flush the negative feelings and help them quiet down. If somebody is disturbed, you could enable them to feel tranquil. On the off chance that somebody feels despair, you could extend trust straight into their heart. You could share and enhance your most joyful sentiments to make an emotional atmosphere of unadulterated satisfaction.

This procedure depends on the hypothesis that an entryway once opened might be ventured through in either bearing. On the off chance that you feel another's feelings, at that point, you have a connection legitimately to their heart. So for what reason should you feel the feeling? Some portion of the reason you get they are communicating that they wear not have any desire to feel that way. So help them feel something better by turning around the feed and anticipating a feeling through the connection rather than just accepting it.

To do this, it is fundamental to develop ammunition stockpile of happiness, tranquillity, peace, confidence and cherishing memories in your brain. To extend a feeling, you need to feel it. To find or gain a couple of experiences, empathy needs to be kept in the cutting edge of your psyche. When have you felt joyful, successfully cheerful? When have you felt so quiet and loosened up that you could have remained as such until the end of time? Construct an information stockpile of these recollections in your psyche. Record them if it causes you to show them. Work on inclination them regularly. This will do some incredible things in a larger number of ways than one.

So on the off chance that you go over somebody whose feelings are shouting for assistance, do the following. Take a full breath and settle on what feeling you wish to extend. In the wellbeing of your psyche, review the memory that inspires your picked feeling. Make the memory as solid as conceivable in the present. Give the feeling of that memory a chance to fill your heart. At the point when your heart is overflowing with your picked feeling, send the abundance enthusiastic vitality you've created towards your objective. Give the vitality a chance to saturate the connection between your souls. Your passionate projection will gradually overpower and change their negative enthusiastic state until it mirrors your inspiration.

- **Showing with Empathy**

Energy streams where feeling goes. Empathy gives a genuine lift with regards to showing the empaths' deepest longings in all actuality. To show, you can utilize your creative mind, you can make a dream board with pictures of what you need, and you can record what you need in the request structure. The majority of that is fine, yet what truly makes it work is the feeling.

The feeling is a widespread language that the universe comprehends at a base level. Sentiments have so much vitality and power in our lives that it just bodes well that they assume such a significant job in showing.

One minimal known favorable position of being an empath is that since we are associated with the core of the universe so personally when we feel something, we feel it into reality. So when you compose your petitions or make your vision sheets, utilize the full intensity of your feelings. Whatever you are drawing into you, feel what it resembles to have it now. Task how astonishing it feels to have what you need most, regardless of whether you don't have it. With regards to showing, empathy is an exceptional blessing!

Being an engaged empath

As a sensitive and empathic individual, there is a lot to be thankful for: you are equipped for encountering lovely enthusiasm and happiness. You can see the comprehensive view on a more profound level. You are sensitive to the magnificence, verse, and energy of life. Your empathy enables you to help other people. You are not hard or closed off or wanton. Your sensitivities enable you to mind, helpless, and mindful. You have a unique relationship to nature. You feel a family relationship with creatures, blossoms, trees, and mists. You might be attracted to the tranquillity of the wild, the calm of the desert, the red shake gorge, the woods, or the boundlessness of the sea. You may move under the full moon and feel her exquisiteness in your body. You realize how to wind up one with the quietness of nature. You need to secure the earth, our mom, and save her valuable assets. Empaths can empathically change themselves, their families, and the remainder of the world.

Empaths speak to another model for authority by being defenseless and solid. They can hugely affect humankind by advancing common comprehension—the way to harmony in our own lives and comprehensively. In any case, such upsets will stick just when the inward enthusiastic and otherworldly work is finished by the progressives. At that point, external positive changes—political, social, and ecological—are conceivable.

Chapter 8: Empathy Revolution: Need of the hour

We live during a time of hyper-independence, a period where an overdose oversimplified self-improvement, have persuaded that the most ideal approach to lead the great life and accomplish human joy, is to seek after our limited personal circumstances, to pursue our wants. Sadly, we have become so selfish that the world is facing a looming crisis. Someone has to take any action; a cure is needed. That cure is empathy.

For a large number of years, humankind's history has been commanded by developing advances that focuses on making tasks easier and provides convenience. Up until now, we have kept away from across the calamity; however, that point is not far away. Be that as it may, as our reality turns out to be increasingly interconnected and our advances progressively coordinated and incredible, we are in peril of losing the capacity to deal with the difficulties that self-serving innovation development makes.

Presently, we as a whole realize that empathy has any kind of effect in our everyday connections. Be it with humans or animals, we see empathy around us. However, the main concern is the rising cases of apathy, cruelty and capitalistic mindset. No doubt, empaths are so overwhelmed all the time. Their ability to communicate is being overloaded with each passing day.

In any case, empathy can accomplish more than assistance in our connections. Compassion can make radical social change. It can give rise to a revolution of which our world is in dire need. What's more, we desperately need this social change because of a developing worldwide empathy deficiency.

Why empathy revolution is needed?

Empathy levels have declined by almost half in the course of the most recent decades. We have overall developed social partitions. In a majority of western nations, the bridge between rich and poor is more prominent today than it was earlier. Simultaneously, over a billion people on the planet are living in poor conditions. Wherever we turn, we see the contentions brought about by religious fundamentalism, ethnic strains, and xenophobia. We desperately need empathy to make the social glue to hold our social orders together and to disintegrate the harmful egoistical attitudes, that is the reason for so much social unrest.

Biologically, our cerebrums are wired for empathy. We are Homo Empathicus. In any case, not very many of us have truly arrived at our full empathic potential. Furthermore, as a general public, we haven't yet truly figured out how to saddle the intensity of empathy, to make social and political change. Initiating a worldwide empathy revolution would do nothing but good to this world.

How can we do it?

Empaths have to prepare our future generations. Since empathy can be educated and learned, it very well may be adapted simply like riding a bicycle or figuring out how to drive a vehicle. It's ideal to learn it when you're youthful. The world's most noteworthy program for training sympathy is the one you can see on the screen here which is known as the Roots of Empathy. It started in Canada, in 1995. An interesting thing about it is that the educator is a child. An infant comes into the study hall, at regular intervals, a similar child for an entire year. What's more, the kid's lounge around the infant and they begin talking to the infant. What's the child thinking, what's the infant feeling, for what reason is the infant crying, for what reason is the infant snickering? They're attempting to relate, into the shoes of the infant. What's more, they at that point utilize that action to begin thinking about empathy on a more extensive scale.

Be that as it may, we can hardly wait for a long time. For these change-producers to develop, we have to turn out to be progressively empathic ourselves and lead the empathic unrest as people, as grown-ups. That is the reason we have to build up an eager creative mind. The most recent brain science research lets us know that on the off chance that you carefully center around another person's sentiments and necessities, that is, feel for them, that expands your ethical worry with them and can spur you to make a move on their sakes.

One of the best empathic travelers in humankind's history, Mahatma Gandhi, indicated that we need to be somewhat yearning about whose shoes we choose to step into. He broadly stated, in a statement called Gandhi's Talisman, he said "At whatever point you are in uncertainty, or when oneself is a lot with you, apply the accompanying test. Review the substance of the least fortunate man who you may have seen and inquire as to whether the progression you think about will be of any utilization to him. At that point, you will discover your questions and yourself dissolving ceaselessly."

Simply envision if that empathic message was on the work area of each financial titan or media noble, or even without anyone else. In any case, Gandhi likewise indicated that we need to propel ourselves considerably further, that we have to identify just with poor people and the feeble, yet additionally venture into the shoes of our adversaries. We, as a whole, need to figure out how to feel for our foes, to build our degrees of resistance, to make us more astute individuals, and furthermore to create more brilliant methodologies of social change.

How would you individuals here today get the chance to meet individuals who are not quite the same as you, and venture into their shoes? Well, that is the reason we have to accomplish something different in the empathy revolution, which is to start our interest. Presently, the vast majority of have lost the interest that we once had in our childhood. We stroll past outsiders consistently, without realizing what's happening in their psyches. We scarcely know our neighbors. We have to develop an interest in outsiders to challenge our partialities and stereotypes. The considerations in other individuals' heads, is the extraordinary apathy that encompasses us. Furthermore, the empaths along with others have to utilize developing discussions with outsiders to enter that obscurity.

We have to start somewhere. To bridge the gap, we could talk to a new person each week. Regardless of whether the individual vacuums the floor in the workplace, or somebody who, you know, you purchase a paper from each day. The significant thing is to get past shallow talk and simply discussing the climate, and discussion about the stuff that truly matters throughout everyday life: love and passing, legislative issues and humanity.

Yet, we additionally need to develop an interest in outsiders on a social level and advance undertakings like the Human Library Movement which you can see up here on the screen. It started around 10 years back in Denmark and the Human Library

Movement is presently spread to more than 20 nations. On the off chance that you go to a Human Library Event, similar to this one in London, what you do, you come and, rather than acquiring a book, as you would do from an ordinary library, you get an individual, for discussion. It may be a Nigerian soul vocalist, or it could be a single parent living off welfare. The fact of the matter is to have discussions with individuals who are concerning you, challenge your generalizations. Simply envision, on the off chance that you sorted out a Human Library Event in your locale, who might you welcome along for individuals from the general population to converse with, to start their interest?

Presently, how would we realize that these discussions and experiences between outsiders, can truly have any kind of effect? History lets us know so. We have to gain from history. We typically consider empathy as something that occurs between people. In any case, empathy can likewise exist on a mass scale, on an aggregate level.

Presently, if you glance through history, there have been snapshots of mass empathic breakdown. Think about the Holocaust, for instance. Be that as it may, there have similarly been snapshots of mass empathic blooming.

We have to make experiences this way, today. Fortunately, they are as of now occurring. In the Middle East, for instance, there is an association called the Parents' Circle. What's more, it does phenomenal grass-roots harmony building ventures. My preferred one, that they did was known as the 'Welcome Peace' phone line. Presently, on the off chance that you are an Israeli, you could telephone this phone free telephone number, and you are put through to an irregular Palestinian outsider. You could converse with them for up to 30 minutes. Palestinians could telephone the number and they were put through to Israelis. In the initial five years of activity, more than one million calls were made on this line.

Simply suppose you could set up one of those telephone lines today among rich and poor or environmental change cynics and environmental change activists. One thing I haven't spoken about, however, is making experiential experiences. Simply suppose we didn't simply have discussions with individuals however we could encounter something of their lives. I think a model of this is an association called 'Exchange in the Dark', which is a one of a kind type of historical center experience where you go into a space for an hour in complete haziness, and a visually impaired guide takes you through to find what it resembles to be denied of your sight for 60 minutes. You do exercises like attempting to purchase foods grown from the ground and you mishandle with your cash. You go into a bistro, attempt and plunk down and drink espresso and, you know, discover how troublesome it is. This exhibition hall experience is uncommonly ground-breaking for individuals, and this association has spread the world over. 'Discourse in the Dark' has shown up in more than 130 urban communities, in 30 nations. Indeed, it's as of late simply opened in Athens, and more than 6 million individuals have experienced its entryways. So we have to make experiential experiences to grow our circles of good concern.

We likewise need to figure out how to tackle innovation. Innovation's consistently been significant in empathic developments. In the battle against subjugation in the late eighteenth century, the innovation that was utilized was the printing press to print blurbs, a huge number of them of what number of African slaves could be fitted on a British slave ship heading off to the Caribbean. This notice prompted mass open objection, petitions and it prompted, in the long run, the cancellation of servitude and the slave exchange itself.

To make it workable for the Sustainability Revolution to win, we need to discover another way going past the extraordinary shafts of the perfect world and oppressed world. If we need to reclassify connections between states, business, and society, we must be available to helpful discourse and molding open worth – a procedure which depends on straightforwardness, responsibility, and respectability, just as incorporating all on-screen characters in the planetary scene.

On the off chance that we don't comprehend that taking a stab at the normal social great is the most ideal approach to spare our living space and ourselves, we will convey the fault for the hardships of the ages to come. Each unrest first occurs in quite a while and hearts. Sympathy, empathy, and solidarity can give the urgent force for the significant and durable difference in the all-inclusive mentality. An Empathy Revolution ought to be viewed as essential for the Sustainability Revolution.

In the previous two decades, the appearance of MRI in neuroscience has created fantastic accomplishments in the investigation of the human mind. Researchers have unfortunately affirmed that individuals naturally will, in general, be egocentric. In any case, fortunately, there is a particular piece of our cerebrum, called the privilege supramarginal gyrus, which is in charge of sympathy and empathy. This region of the mind makes it feasible for us to disengage the view of ourselves from that of others. Additionally, the privilege supramarginal gyrus is brilliant to the point that it can perceive an absence of empathy and autocorrect it. The demonstrated neuroplasticity of our cerebrum guarantees that our ability for sympathy is never fixed. By intentionally placing ourselves in another person's shoes, we can fortify the pliability of our neural systems and impressively improve our potential for sympathy and empathy.

Empathy is our responsibility

Being empathic isn't useful for our kindred individuals yet similarly serves our circumstance. Neuroscientists have demonstrated that exceptionally empathic individuals feel increasingly satisfied, are progressively positive, alert and idealistic, and furthermore, for the most part, will, in general, live more joyful and longer lives than their egocentric partners!

With regards to the corporate world, it would imply that those organizations that see aggregate enthusiasm as their own, and are guided by the standards of open worth and social great, would thus, by implication, be working for their bit of leeway and could just make win-win circumstances.

In our worldwide world with all its worldwide entertainers, areas, networks, systems and developments, is there any valid reason why we wouldn't try to accomplish and spread worldwide compassion also? The Empathy Revolution could unquestionably carry us a lot nearer to the worldwide execution of the Sustainability Revolution. In this way, let us enact the privilege supramarginal gyrus of our minds and show signs of improvement world for all!

Today, the innovation we have to consider is long-range informal communication advances, computerized advances. Presently, we realize that they can be incredible. We realize that during the Arab

Spring and in the Occupy development, long-range interpersonal communication stages helped spread amazing feelings, similar to outrage and empathy. Someone could snap a picture of a young lady called Nedā, shot in the city of Tehran, and inside hours a large number of individuals around the globe knew her name, about her family, what her identity was, and went on to the lanes to challenge at state fierceness.

In any case, you likewise need to perceive that cutting edge advancements, computerized innovations, have a risk to them. Since, most interpersonal interaction stages have been intended for the proficient trade of data, not for the trading of closeness and sympathy. They will in general advance, once in a while, shallow connections. There's a peril that they advance the amount of the associations we make instead of the quality. They will in general associate us with individuals who are especially similar to us, who offer our preferences in music or movies. So we have to make another age of person to person communication advances, which spotlight on extending profound empathic association and interfacing us with outsiders.

Be that as it may, just as this, we have to figure out how to be empathic pioneers. Since we are for the most part pioneers, we as a whole have authoritative reaches, regardless of whether it's in schools or the work environment, in places of worship or network associations. We can take a lead from renowned pioneers, for example, Nelson Mandela who understood, that in the progress from Apartheid, it was indispensable to attempt to make sympathy and common comprehension among highly contrasting South Africans. He is one of the most famous and respected empathic personalities so far. These personalities did what others hesitated to do- being empathic.

So those are the fixings to begin an empathy insurgency. Socrates broadly said that to carry on with an astute and great life, we have to 'know thyself'. What's more, we have generally imagined that this implies peering inside yourself, looking at your very own soul. We have to adjust thoughtfulness, with what we call-- introspection. Outrospection is finding what your identity is, and how to live by venturing outside yourself, and glancing through the eyes of other individuals and finding other individuals' universes. Empathy is a definitive fine art for the time of outrospection.

Presently empathy, as an idea, is better known today than at any crossroads in mankind's history. It's on the lips of legislators and neuroscientists, business pioneers and spiritual gurus. We need to accomplish something other than discussion about empathy or searching for it on the internet. We need to transform empathy into a type of social activity. We have to outfit its capacity for social and political change. That is how we will make an upheaval of human connections in the 21st century.

Empathy revolution is the need of the hour. It's something which our world would be thankful for eternity. Selflessness is the tool which humans must learn to make use of. No, empathy is not a weakness; it's the biggest strength one can ever possess.

Be an empath and see the happiness unfolding around yourself.

Conclusion

Being sensitive or empathic is something with which quite a few people are blessed. Sadly, the world is not understanding the importance of empathy.

Nowadays, no one seems to be happy. Don't our hearts bleed when we see our near and dear ones in pain? Don't we feel like extending our hand, pulling them into a hug and tell them that everything will be fine? These things are instinctive. They are physical and present. They are going on this moment and you can feel it in your bones. Yet it equally tough to find someone to lean upon when the world is slowly becoming desensitized to the emotions. Feeling sympathy is common, while empathetic gestures are increasingly becoming uncommon.

A change has to come.

Empaths have to start from somewhere. To bridge the gap, they could talk to a new person each week. Regardless of whether the individual vacuums the floor in the workplace, or somebody who, you know, you purchase a paper from each day. The significant thing is to get past shallow talk and simply discussing the climate, and discussion about the stuff that truly matters throughout everyday life: love and passing, legislative issues and humanity.

Social developments have led to the mechanization of everything, even emotions. Everything is guarded, a lie that we tell ourselves and others. For example, take social media-- we scroll and scroll, like and comment on cute videos and emotional stories of struggling human beings. However, how many of us would reach out to others to help those who are in distress? This is the moment when we have to realize that humanity needs to be awakened again. The emotions which we have been suppressing to fit into the crowd needs to burn with passion again. It is a rallying call for us to decorate their defensive layer, get our weapons, and stand up to the foe at their entryway. Our enemy is none other than our insensitivity. It needs to be taken care of. The world needs healing; it needs the touch of love and genuine empathy. It needs healers.

Here in this book, you will get to know more about Empath Healing, abilities, strengths, weaknesses, and much more. This information is essential for us to embrace our true, emotional selves as that would allow to clear our biases and become better human beings in the process. Feeling our inner love and those of others isn't a weakness. It will build up this world. In the time when empathy is buried deep inside somewhere and shallowness is riding with its head high, healers can be the saviors. If you feel you are the one, then do not hesitate to take charge. Do not be afraid to be charitable when it comes to servicing the humankind because this is precisely what we need now. And you need to protect yourself as well because without protecting yourself you cannot help others. It is essential to take a stand for yourself or else it will be too late-- for you and the worl

CPSIA information can be obtained
at www.ICGtesting.com
Printed in the USA
LVHW010415130121
676360LV00005B/276